SOLO FOR HORNE

The biography of Kenneth Horne by Norman Hackforth

ANGUS & ROBERTSON · PUBLISHERS

Angus & Robertson · Publishers
London · Sydney · Melbourne
Singapore · Manila

*First published by Angus & Robertson
(U.K.) Ltd. 1976
Copyright © Norman Hackforth 1976
ISBN 0 207 95650 2
Made and printed in Great Britain
by Northumberland Press Ltd., Gateshead
Book designed by
Peggy and Drummond Chapman*

DEDICATION

To all those innumerable people
who counted him their friend,
I affectionately dedicate this book.

CONTENTS

Acknowledgements

A GREAT many people have contributed, freely and affectionately, a number of stories and incidents in this book. I am grateful to them all. I have kept a record of my many correspondents, and I hope I have not inadvertently omitted any names.

My sincere thanks are due, firstly, to Kenneth Horne's relatives and close friends.

To his sister, Mrs Ruth Gordon, his brother, Mr Ronald Cozens-Hardy Horne, his cousin Lord Pilkington, and his step-daughter, Mrs Susan Montague, my principle and most generous sources of information.

To Kenneth's and my own mutual friends in broadcasting, Barry Took, Richard Murdoch, Sam Costa, Maurice Denham, Kenneth Williams, Betty Marsden, Bill Pertwee, John Ellison, Paul Jennings, Bobby Jaye, Humphrey Barclay, Daphne Padell, Joyce Grenfell, Anne Croft, Graham Tennant.

To His Grace The Duke of Newcastle, Lady Mary Clinton-Hope, Mrs John Beavis, Miss Joyce Davis, Mrs Kathleen Bryant, Mrs Christine Bennett, Mrs Mollie Millest, Mrs Constance Lea, Mr Barrie Heath, Mr Ralph Hewson, Mr Roger Swinburne-Johnson, Mr

ACKNOWLEDGEMENTS

Edward Wilkinson, Mr Edmund King, Mr Charles Cripps, Mr Alan Hess, Mr H. W. Austin, Mr Pat Newman, Mr Robert Luff, Mr Alan Gibson, Mr Paul Jennens, Mr Arthur Katz, Lord Mancroft, Mr Joe Friel, Mr Percy Millea, Sir Jan Lewando, Mr David C. Mackenzie, Mr R. P. S. Bache, Miss Kay Bagley, Mrs Marjorie Davies, Mr G. A. Hepworth, Mr Richard Bright, Mr Ronald Mercer, Mr Geoffrey Tulip, Mr W. J. Dawson, Mrs Gertrude Thompson, Mr Geoffrey Ashwell, Mr Desmond Seaton-Reid, Mrs Jane Page, Mr John Dean, Mrs Margaret Lisney, Mr John Collins, Mr A. N. W. Griffiths, Mr C. G. Allen, Mr C. A. Hill, The Hon. Mrs Talbot-Price, Mrs Heather Cavell, Mr T. H. Drury, Mr D. H. Ainsley, Mr Michael Ashfield, Mr Fred Leadbetter, Mrs Ada Lapworth, Mr J. Lawton, Miss E. Miller, Mrs Pamela Massingham.

I am also indebted to Hodder & Stoughton Ltd., for permission to quote from 'The Life of Charles Silvester Horne', by W. B. Selbie.

Picture acknowledgements

The author and publishers wish to thank the Horne family for their kind permission to use personal pictures in this book.
Other copyright illustrations appear by courtesy of: B.B.C., 18, 36, 37, 38, 39, 40; Triplex (*New York Times*) 23; George Dallison, 20; Central Office of Information, 26; *T.V. Times*, 32; London News Agency Photos, 33.

1 "many giants..."

I CAN almost see him looking over my shoulder, with that irrepressible mobility in his face, as if he was always one jump ahead of you thinking up the next gag. And, when you fed him the right line, *zoom*, out it would come, and I can't remember many times when it wasn't a good one!

So, embarking upon this slightly alarming venture of trying to tell something of his life story, I ask:

'Well Ken, what shall I write about?'

And he replies: 'If I were you I should right about turn!'

There may be some of his better gags, as we go along. They were mostly pretty simple stuff, but so endearingly delivered, so meticulously timed, that I find it hard to believe that anybody failed to find them funny.

But this is just affectionate reminiscence. One could go on like this for hours; because the next best thing to talking to Kenneth is talking about him.

I am happily able to say that I knew him. He was my friend; and that was really something. But I daresay you feel that you knew him too. And, if you ever listened to him once on the radio you probably also counted him as your friend.

However, perhaps you would like to know a little more about him; so let's start at the beginning.

Charles Kenneth Horne was born on February 27th, 1907, the seventh, and youngest child of the Reverend Charles Silvester Horne and his wife. Silvester Horne was the youngest son of Charles Horne, of Newport, Shropshire, who had started life as a Congregationalist clergyman, but, with failing health, resigned from the ministry, and became the editor of the local newspaper.

Silvester seems to have inherited a talent for preaching, which he began to practice even in his teens; and, dedicated to making the Church his career, he went first to Glasgow University, where he took his M.A. degree, before going on, with a scholarship, as one of the first batch of students to the newly founded Mansfield College, Oxford, where he read Theology.

Even before he had completed his studies at Mansfield, he was invited by the Congregational Church to become Minister of the parish of Allen Street, Kensington, one of the principal Free Churches, and certainly one of the wealthiest in London.

Doctor Fairbairn, the Principal of Mansfield, arranged for him to travel round the world at the end of his time at Oxford, and he returned in time for his ordination to the Ministry, and took up his appointment at the age of twenty-four. He was clearly a spellbinding preacher, at the start of a brilliant career.

Three years later, in 1892, he married Katharine, eldest daughter of Sir Herbert Cozens-Hardy Q.C., an eminent barrister, and one of Silvester Horne's most fervent supporters in the Church, who later became the first Baron Cozens-Hardy of Letheringsett, when in 1907 he was appointed Master of the Rolls.

The seven children of the marriage were:- a daughter, Dorothy; a son, Oliver; a daughter, Bridget; a daughter, Joan; a son, Ronald; a daughter, Ruth; and lastly, Charles Kenneth. With her father's elevation to the peerage, Katharine became The Honourable Mrs Silvester Horne.

She had been raised in a sheltered comfortable home, and she was undoubtedly a highly cultured lady; yet, on her marriage to this dynamic man of God, she clearly devoted her life unquestioningly to him, regardless of consideration for her own environment.

By 1903 he felt that his work at Allen Street was done, and he was persuaded that there was a new challenge for him to meet in moving to a red-brick chapel in Tottenham Court Road called Whitefields Tabernacle, which was in a neglected and dilapidated condition. He installed his family in a small house in Ampthill Square, at the back of Tottenham Court Road, where first Ruth, and then Kenneth were born.

This was a far cry from the sheltered gentility of Kensington. It was a tough district of London, very much on the wrong side of the tracks, in an area of extreme poverty.

Silvester Horne worked first on the restoration and refurbishing of Whitefields, which he was determined to transform into 'a great centre of Christian influence and activity'. He wasn't content just with religious services. He wanted an adult school, a library, club-rooms, a lounge, a canteen, cooking and sewing classes, choirs and bands, endless activity all through the week. And he got it!

The family was raised in Congregationalist principles, and that this was no hardship is shown by the following extract from a biography of Silvester Horne, contributed by his eldest daughter Dorothy.

'Those winning qualities which made my father so deeply loved by all who knew him found their happiest expression in his home life.... When his key sounded in the front-door, there was always a stampede in the nursery, and we almost fell downstairs in our excitement to be first to give him a welcoming hug. I think the reason why children adored him so whole-heartedly was his entire absence of superiority and aloofness. Although he could be stern when there was any question of wrong-doing, he naturally met us children as a friend and an equal. We were never in the least afraid of him, but our love for him made us terribly afraid of doing anything which would make him sorry.

'It would be difficult to imagine a happier childhood than ours. Religious teaching, if teaching it could be called, was a thing of joy. He did not believe in the continual "Don't", which has made religion seem harsh to some children. We learnt our religion in positive terms through the love of nature, the love of each other, and the desire for service which our father and mother taught us. Sunday was always a favourite day with us, not only because father was usually at home, but because the spirit of the day was a conspicuously glad one.'

From the very outset he transformed Whitefields

into a national institution. He produced a banner depicting a knight in armour, which hung on the facade. He erected arc-lamps to floodlight the building, against which the pub on the opposite side of the road paled into insignificance; and when it ultimately went out of business he took over the building to accommodate the ever expanding needs of his church.

People flocked to his services to hear him preach. He emptied all the surrounding churches, and he held three services each Sunday.

Mrs Horne with her seven children, attended by their nanny, came to the morning service, and sat always in their own pew at the back of the church. It seems hard to believe that, with Silvester in full cry from the pulpit there was the slightest inattention, but there were moments when even Mama's concentration wandered a little. She once confessed to Ruth, years later, that she would occupy herself by biting her initials, K.M.H., in the top of the pew in front, over which her head was bowed in prayer.

'You *couldn't* have done!' said Ruth, at the same time conscious that her mother never told a lie in her life.

'I did,' she replied, 'though I will admit that the K. was rather difficult.'

This autographed pew in front of the Horne family was occupied by grandfather Cozens-Hardy, who travelled the considerable distance from his home in Ladbroke Grove to Whitefields each Sunday, to hear his son-in-law preach. The children were all devoted to him, he was a lovely man. It seems that, when their first baby-teeth were dropping out, he offered them sixpence a tooth for each one presented to him. Sunday church being the one regular occasion on which they saw him, Ruth and Kenneth used to work hard on any potential tooth during the week, to try and get it out by Sunday. They would then place the tooth in a matchbox, and furtively smuggle it forward to grandfather during the prayers. And always, faithfully, back would come a sixpence in the matchbox. Since the going rate of pocket-money was then twopence a week, it is surprising that they were not both completely toothless long before their time.

On Sunday afternoons, Whitefields was given over to the Men's Meeting, as much a dissertation on general affairs of the day as a religious service. After the first few years, there was an enrolled congregation of fifteen hundred men, and they queued to get in to these meetings. Silvester did not always speak himself, but persuaded prominent politicians and writers to come as guest speakers. Bernard Shaw came; so too did Jerome K. Jerome.

The Sunday evening service was the most popular of the day. Billed to start at 7.00 p.m., by six o'clock a board would be placed outside the door with the single word 'FULL'. During the next hour a voluntary orchestra would play musical selections. Sometimes a young organist would come to give a recital. His name was George Thalben-Ball. As seven o'clock came, a hush descended over the entire church, as they waited for the entrance of the magnetic personality whom many had travelled miles to hear.

Silvester Horne's industry was phenomenal. All these ambitious projects and improvements at Whitefields had to be paid for, and to raise the money required he travelled extensively throughout this country and on the Continent, on a series of intensive lecture and preaching tours.

Politically, he was dedicated to the Liberal Party, and gave unstinting services during election campaigns, in support of as many contesting candidates as possible. Finally, in 1910, he himself fought an election, and was returned to Parliament as Liberal M.P. for Ipswich. This step was rather frowned upon by the Deacons (his superiors in the Church), but he wrote:

'Nothing will induce me to give up Whitefields. But I do not believe that the House of Commons need unmake one spiritually, nor Whitefields unfit one for things secular.'

Another of his early letters from the House of Commons was to his mother:

'I felt I must write a line to you from this historic house, to assure you that I am actually here. A few minutes ago I made an affirmation of everlasting loyalty to the King and the Constitution. I sincerely hope that means loyalty to the people, and especially to the poor.'

'The poor' were of constant concern to him.

Silvester had promised to remain at Whitefields for a period of ten years, which, in 1913, was drawing to a close. His future was somewhat unresolved, largely on account of his health which had never been good. Even as early as 1895 he had suffered the first of three nervous breakdowns, but he continued to drive himself heedlessly. He wrote in his diary on April 15th, 1897:

'Today I am thirty-two years old, and the last two years have been somewhat painful ones, despite the sunshine that has come into them from the love of friends. It is far from easy to acquiesce in a medical verdict which would impose upon one that very hardest of duties, the duty of half-a-life. It is curious how hard such a duty seems ... However, it is open to me to disbelieve the doctors.'

Little was he to know that, in expressing this philosophy ten years before the birth of his youngest son Kenneth, that Kenneth himself was to voice almost identical sentiments some seventy years later!

Asked, didn't he think he should take things more easily, Silvester replied, probably with rather more irony than he realized:

'There's too much to do; and the difference between a grave and a groove is only one of depth. You might as well be in one as the other!'

It was clearly becoming impossible for him to continue to work at the tremendous pressure which Whitefields and his parliamentary work entailed.

In the course of his travels around the country, he had found in his beloved county of Shropshire, a large family house, called The White House, at Church Stretton, and he and Katharine had bought it, as the next family home when he moved on from Whitefields.

It was a beautifully situated country house, with nine bedrooms (which indeed they needed), a large hall, library and drawing-room, and a long verandah looking out on to a large garden with two grass tennis-courts. They moved there in the summer of 1913.

8

Another entry in his diary read:

'The last doctor's report is that I have one permanently damaged kidney. It does no work, the ne'er-do-well! But that is not the worst of it. Such is the solidarity of the body corporate that the whole suffers, and must suffer, for its neglect. It is a very pretty parable, and would sound more admirable in a sermon than it does out of one.'

That summer he wrote to Joan, away at boarding-school:

'Of course we miss you terribly here in Church Stretton. Tom has hacked up the whole potato patch, and now they repose in the cellar, and one enormous one that was roasted in its jacket reposes, wonderful to relate, inside Kenneth. He absolutely gorged it, and then announced that he would soon be like "The Little Stodger" ... I have finished my new book and am now about to write the lectures for America.'

The lectures for America were the result of an invitation he had just received from Yale University to go there in the Spring of 1914, to deliver a series of lectures on The History of Preaching.

There was some misgiving about him undertaking this venture; the doctors told him he must, above all, avoid over-exertion, but it was felt that the sea voyage would do him good.

So, the following March, accompanied by his wife he set off on what was in fact his third visit to America, leaving the family in the care of their beloved Nanny May, who (with the exception only of Dorothy) had seen them all into the world, and been with them for nearly twenty years.

The visit to Yale was an unqualified success. They went on by train to Niagara, where, on May 2nd, they embarked on a ship to cross Lake Ontario to visit Toronto, where Silvester was to address a large meeting.

As the ship entered Toronto harbour, he was walking on deck with Katharine when he suddenly fell. She held him in her arms, but even before any help could reach him he was dead.

He was just forty-nine years old.

His body was taken from the ship to the house of Mr N. W. Rowell K.C., where they were to have stayed. The meeting Silvester was to have addressed became instead the first of many memorial services. The Rowell family were endlessly kind, and took charge of all arrangements. Poor Katharine, grief stricken but admirably composed, embarked a few days later on a sad solitary journey for England, bringing with her the body of her beloved husband, which was laid to rest in the cemetery at Church Stretton.

United more than ever in their grief, the family resumed their lives, with The White House as the unifying centre. Dorothy wrote:

'The shock of his death came on us like a thunderbolt from a clear sky. We could only find comfort in the knowledge that our relations with him had been perfect, and that his presence would continue to fill our home, as it had always done.'

She was just twenty-one, in her last year at Lady Margaret Hall, Oxford. She took a good degree, joined the Civil Service, and later became an Inspector at the Board of Trade, before marrying. Her husband, in the

Diplomatic Service, was in later years Sir Archibald Gordon, C.M.G., whose younger brother, Douglas, in 1942 married Ruth.

Oliver, nineteen at the time of his father's death, was still at New College, Oxford. In August of that year he joined the Army, and went right through the War.

Bridget, at seventeen, was not quite grown up. She was a home-loving girl, and not intent upon a career.

Katharine Horne assumed the upbringing of her younger children with great authority tempered always with affection and humour.

Sunday was a day of rest. They all went to church, and in the evening they sang hymns, which the children chose themselves. Kenneth and Ruth preferred the gory ones of Moody and Sankey:

'*Many giants great and tall*
Stalking through the land
Headlong to the earth would fall
When met by Daniel's band.'

It seems that their mother was the first person to jazz hymn tunes, and had 'a great swing arrangement of "Jerusalem the Golden"'.

Kenneth went, for the next six years, to a preparatory school in Shrewsbury, before going on to St Georges School, Harpenden, Hertfordshire, where all the children were educated. This was undoubtedly one of the earliest coeducational schools in this country, and the choice of it is indicative of their parents' progressive outlook.

Idyllically happy school holidays were spent at home.

"MANY GIANTS..."

It was at The White House that Kenneth first started to play tennis, later to become one of his best sports. They organized the Church Stretton tournaments, which were played on their own and their neighbours' courts, and were three day events of some importance. They had a fairly high-powered family four, with Joan, Ronald, Ruth and Kenneth. They played golf over the hills, with one club each (and seldom more than one ball!). They bicycled for miles, they camped in the local valleys; and in the winters there were the special Christmas plays, written and produced by the family, and enthusiastically performed by them on Christmas Eve, a continuation of a tradition which their father had instituted many years earlier. It is clear, from the scripts of some of these Christmas plays, that there was a strong histrionic creative talent running right through the family; from 'The Hermit of Helmeth', in 1919, to 'Caravanserai', in 1932, with the programmes which were specially designed for them.

It would be irrelevant to reproduce them in detail, for they are understandably parochial and topical of their day. In 1921, for example, there were comic references to crossword-puzzles, which first appeared in England that year. But the most notable thing about these scripts is the tremendous industry and passionate enthusiasm which went into their production. They were meticulously typed; parody lyrics were written to current popular songs; scenery was specially painted. Costumes were devised and adapted from Mother's 'marvellous store of dressing-up clothes'. These elaborate productions were far removed from the average family charades. There was, of course, a preponderance

of rather 'in' jokes, pertaining to friends and neighbours in Church Stretton. All the family had nicknames, for which there is no remembered explanation
of origin, though they survived right through their
lives. Dorothy was 'Doge', Oliver 'Hoax', Bridget
'Boge', Joan 'Jarkis', Ronald 'Plackus', Kenneth 'Sparg',
and Ruth 'Puth' (pronounced inexplicably as in 'Ar-
buthnot') which Kenneth called her all his life. Ronald,
Ruth and Kenneth had a special language of their own,
in which they were able to converse for long periods
without being understood by anybody else.

Ronald, when he grew up, studied Law, no doubt
inspired by his illustrious grandfather. He went to
Balliol College, Oxford, where he took a degree, and
was called to the Bar in 1927. He moved into chambers
at number seven New Square, Lincoln's Inn, which
for many years had been occupied by Lord Cozens-
Hardy (who had worked at the same desk industri-
ously wielding his quill pen!), where he continued to
practise for the whole of his professional life.

Ronald's qualification as a barrister was understandably an event of great importance in the family, and
in celebration of it the next Christmas production had
a strong legal flavour.

Many years later, Kenneth told the story of the time
they were all sitting round the piano singing *The
Honeysuckle and the Bee*, and it occurred to him that
the words 'Mount Popocatepetl' exactly fitted the
rhythm of the music. He said to Ronald:

'I bet you can't write new words to that song, starting
with the line "I am Mount Popocatepetl", and rhym-
ing it.'

Ronald looked at him patronizingly.

'Give me five minutes,' he said.

In three he was back. 'Play me the tune,' he said to Ruth at the piano. Ruth went into the introduction, and he sang:

> *'I am Mount Popocatepetl,*
> *You will agree*
> *When I erupt I scatter metal*
> *Over land and sea.*
> *Don't let your molten matter settle*
> *On my vertebrae!*
> *It's safer far to pat a nettle*
> *Than to sit on me.'*

Ken didn't have it all his own way. The talent competition was pretty keen!

2 all play and no work

IT has been difficult to gather information about Kenneth's schooldays, though he was undoubtedly very popular at St Georges with his tremendous sense of humour, his fine singing voice, and his passion for Gilbert & Sullivan, which continued throughout his life.

He was something of a hero to Geoffrey Ashwell, five years his junior, who admired his achievements as an athlete.

Gertrude Hind-Smith was in the same form, and moved up the school with him, and together they achieved the joint distinction of being Captains of Games.

He eventually rose to the position of 'Head Pupil' (a title which seems properly indicative of a lack of sex discrimination!). Years later he remarked to an interviewer that he never quite made 'Head Girl!'

A sport in which he also excelled was lacrosse. There was an annual 'Girls v. Boys' match, which was a high spot of the school year. 'Once Kenneth got the ball, no one had any hope of catching him from one end of the field to the other.'

ALL PLAY AND
NO WORK

Two of his school nicknames were 'Dickie' ('Tit-Willow' perhaps?) and 'Curly', on account of his abundant crop of curly black hair.

An early love in his life was Anne Moulsdale, who was not a pupil at St Georges, but was at boarding-school at 'St Leonard's', St Andrews, Fife, where he used to write to her, and send completely illicit boxes of chocolates. A pretty big deal at the age of fourteen! This friendship survived for quite a few years, and she never forgot a profound thought of Chairman Horne, which maintained that: 'It is better to keep silent and be thought a fool than to speak and remove all doubt.'

Kenneth left St Georges at seventeen, the last of the long line of Hornes at the school. They had clearly made an impression upon this establishment, because, years later, the governors decided to knock down the partitions between some of the classrooms, and to name the result 'Horne Hall'. Later in his life, Kenneth himself became a governor of the school.

He was next sent to the London School of Economics, which his mother had undoubtedly decided was to be the conclusion of his formal education and a training to equip him for a career. Kenneth accepted this decision with equanimity, if not with much enthusiasm, for he had always had a healthy respect for his mother's wishes, which he would not have dreamed of questioning.

Two of his tutors at the L.S.E. were Hugh Dalton and Stephen Leacock. One might think that the latter had some influence in moulding Kenneth's brilliant sense of comedy, but his own opinion of this illustrious gentleman was: 'One of the most boring lecturers I ever came across'!

In addition to his grandfather, Lord Cozens-Hardy, as one of the family's benefactors, they also had another, to whom Kenneth in particular had reason to be eternally grateful, his uncle Austin Pilkington, who was married to his mother's sister, Hope Cozens-Hardy, thus relating the Horne family to the famous glass manufacturers Pilkington Brothers of St Helens. Uncle Austin, who had a family of two daughters and three sons of his own, nevertheless seems to have been particularly fond of Kenneth, and concerned for his future. His son Harry, two years older than Kenneth, was at that time at Magdalene College, Cambridge, a fact of which Kenneth was understandably highly envious. He loathed the London School of Economics, and meeting Harry and hearing of all the heady delights of life at Cambridge, he wished fervently that he too could go there.

So great-hearted Uncle Austin granted his wish, and arranged a place for him at Magdalene. His last term at the L.S.E. was devoted to frantic concentrated cramming. He somehow managed to achieve a minimal shaky pass in Little-go, and in 1925 duly arrived at Magdalene.

His rooms in college looked out on to Bridge Street, a busy main thoroughfare and a bus-route, with open-top buses. It didn't take much to distract Kenneth's attention from his studies, but it seems the buses were a source of constant fascination, particularly when one of them, stopped on the corner of Chesterton Road, carried on the front seat of the top deck a rather pretty girl. Two days later, staring out of his window again to relieve the excruciating boredom of his paper on political economy, there was the same girl, on the same seat, of presumably the same bus! It was too much for him. He ran from the room, down to the quadrangle, grabbed his bicycle and followed the bus. About a mile on, as the bus slowed for a stop at the bottom of Sidney Street, the girl got up and started down the stairs. At the same time, a young man emerged from inside the bus, greeted her on the platform and helped her to alight. Kenneth boggled. Then he recognized the young man as a friend of his, 'Phiz' Brown, an undergraduate at Christ's. Kenneth stopped his bicycle as they left the bus. Phiz could hardly fail to see him.

'Oh, hullo Ken.'

'Why, Phiz, fancy seeing you!' He looked expectantly at the girl.

'Oh,' said Phiz, 'this is Marjorie French. Kenneth Horne.'

'Miss French, delighted! Why don't we all have some coffee?'

'I can't,' said Phiz. 'I'm late for a lecture as it is.'

'Too bad!' said Kenneth. 'How about you, Miss French?'

'Well, —I—'

'Splendid! Be seeing you, Phiz! Come along, let's go in here.'

Marjorie French was seventeen. Her father was very strict, and she had to be home by nine o'clock at night, which was 'very difficult'. But she had a conveniently married elder sister, who lived in London, and during the vacation she went to stay with her. Kenneth took

ALL PLAY AND
NO WORK

her to a theatre, and afterwards to the Café de Paris. A
fleeting romance, but a sweet one!

This was the culmination of probably the happiest
time of his life. By now he had become a first-class all-
round athlete, and Cambridge provided unlimited
scope for all the many sports which he loved. He was a
fine rugby player; he played for Magdalene, and only
narrowly missed being capped for the University. He
played cricket; was excellent at squash; he was a pretty
good golfer, although he modestly claimed later that
he played it only 'for his own amazement'. He also
shone in athletics, particularly as a hurdler, and had
the distinction of pacing the great Lord Burleigh, one
of the most distinguished hurdlers of this century. He
was good enough at tennis to be included in the University team, as a doubles player, for which he got a
half-blue. He partnered the great H. W. ('Bunny')
Austin, whom he had met some years earlier in 1921,
when they were both competing in the Schoolboys
Championship at Queens Club, which Bunny Austin
won, largely due to Kenneth's tremendous encouragement and faith in him.

With all these many activities, it is hardly surprising that he found little or no time to devote to academic
work. He frankly admitted that, in his entire time at
university, he attended precisely seven lectures; which
may constitute something of a record, but was fairly
reprehensible.

In fairness it should be pointed out that, in April
1926, his 'studies' were interrupted by the General
Strike, which temporarily closed the university. This,
however, provided him with an opportunity to come

to London and become a volunteer bus-driver. This brief interlude was marked by two events. The first, when an enraged woman threw a hair-brush at him. The second, when he obligingly diverted from the prescribed bus-route to drop several passengers at their homes.

In the long vacation of 1926, the team of the Cambridge University Lawn Tennis Club was invited to visit Germany for a series of tournaments and exhibition matches. This team consisted of Russell Young, Kenneth Horne, Bunny Austin, Bill Powell and Jack Baines, and a memorable time seems to have been had by all.

According to Bunny Austin: 'Kenneth had the joyful gift of turning every occasion into a party, and every party into an occasion.'

Bunny, Kenneth and 'Rusty' Young were always around together, and Kenneth suggested they should form a club. They were dining together and, in search of inspiration for a name for the club, Ken consulted the menu. He noticed that most of the dishes had long German names, but, at the bottom of the menu was a short word which took his fancy, 'obst', which they discovered was the German for 'fruit'.

So it was agreed that it should be The Obst Club, (with Obst mispronounced as in 'lobster'!), and the three members would be designated as 'Ein, Zwei and Drei'. They next designed a club tie, which they had made-up to their special order. It displayed silver bowls of fruit on a green ground, with the separate numbers 1. 2. and 3. Bunny Austin has his to this day. There seem to have been several reunions of the club members over the years. In 1931, Bunny received a typical nonsense-letter from Kenneth (p. 22). The club continued to meet at irregular intervals right up to 1961.

Kenneth returned to Cambridge for the October term of 1927, when nemesis finally caught up with him. His tutor summoned him and sadly informed him that the standard of his work had fallen irretrievably short of what was expected of an undergraduate, and since he had failed to satisfy the examiners it seemed fruitless for him to remain at the University. He was quietly sent down at the end of term.

This rather disreputable episode in his life tended to be glossed-over by some of his chroniclers in later years, and treated somewhat in the nature of 'a jolly jape'. After all, it was 'nothing to be ashamed of', just *not working* at Cambridge?' He was 'a jolly good sportsman', and so on. At the time, Uncle Austin didn't take quite such a light-hearted forgiving attitude. What Kenneth seems to have overlooked is that, but for the indulgence and generosity of Uncle Austin, he would never have experienced all the glories, the glamour, the immeasurable advantages of Cambridge, and that all Uncle Austin had hoped for in return was some minimal attention to the main object of the exercise, which was gaining a degree. As a director of Pilkingtons, he had it in his gift to nominate Kenneth for a job with the Company, in the hope that, in course of time, he might prove himself worthy of consideration for a directorship. He now declined to make this nomination.

This was a very serious state of affairs for Kenneth, and probably his first encounter with the stern realities

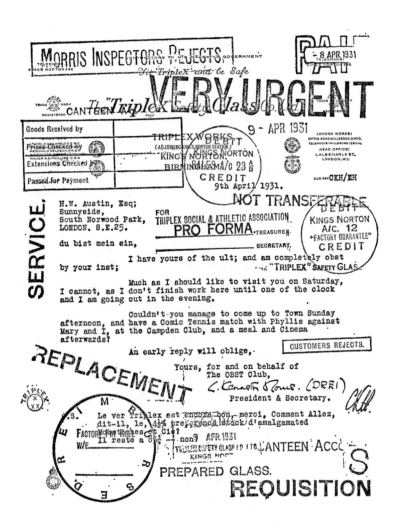

MORRIS INSPECTORS REJECTS.

"Triplex" Safety Glass

CANTEEN

VERY URGENT

RAI

− 8 APR 1931

9 − APR 1931

Goods Received by	
Prices Checked by	
Extensions Checked by	
Passed for Payment	

TRIPLEX WORKS
(ADJOINING KINGS NORTON STATION.)
KING'S NORTON
BIRMINGHAM

DEBIT
KINGS NORTON
SALES A/C 23
CREDIT
9th April 1931.

LONDON WORKS:
HYTHE ROAD, WILLESDEN, N.W.10.
HEAD OFFICE:
1, ALBEMARLE ST.,
LONDON, W.1

OUR REF. CKH/EH

NOT TRANSFERABLE

DEBIT
KINGS NORTON
A/C. 12
"FACTORY GUARANTEE"
CREDIT

SERVICE.

H.W. Austin, Esq;
Sunnyside,
South Norwood Park,
LONDON. S.E.25.

FOR
TRIPLEX SOCIAL & ATHLETIC ASSOCIATION.
PRO FORMA.

TREASURER.
SECRETARY.

du bist mein ein,

I have yours of the ult; and am completely obst
by your inst;

"TRIPLEX" SAFETY GLASS

Much as I should like to visit you on Saturday,
I cannot, as I don't finish work here until one of the clock
and I am going out in the evening.

Couldn't you manage to come up to Town Sunday
afternoon, and have a Comic Tennis match with Phyllis against
Mary and I, at the Campden Club, and a meal and Cinema
afterwards?

An early reply will oblige.

CUSTOMERS REJECTS.

REPLACEMENT

Yours, for and on behalf of
The OBST Club,

L. Kenneth Rowe. (DREI)
President & Secretary.

Le ver Triplex est encora bon, merci. Comment Allez,
dit-il, le 4½% preference stock d'amalgamated
FACTORY manches et Cie?
W/E Il reste a 86? — non? APR 1931
TRIPLEX SAFETY GLASS LTD. CANTEEN ACC
KINGS NORT

PREPARED GLASS.

REQUISITION

of life. Apart from an impressive record as an all-round sportsman, and an endearing personality, he had little to offer, and the year 1927 was not the easiest time for any young man to try to embark upon a career.

Uncle Austin relented to the extent of mentioning his nephew to a certain Colonel Clare, a friend of his who was a director of a firm called The Triplex Safety Glass Company Ltd., important customers of Pilkingtons; though he asked no special favours, and left it entirely to the discretion of the Company to decide whether they might be able to find any employment at all for this renegade youth.

3 cut glass

BEAR with me a moment, if you will, while I tell you briefly the story of the discovery of safety glass, which I have come across in the course of these enquiries, and, I think, is quite a romance in itself; somewhat along the lines of that much elaborated account of Fleming and penicillin (the spilling of the formaldehyde on to the cheese) which has always struck me as rather far-fetched.

It seems that a French scientist named Benedictus, early in the twentieth century, placed a solution of cellulose-acetate in a glass flask which he left on a shelf in his laboratory for several months. One day he accidentally knocked over the flask which fell to the floor. Unlike that earlier scientist, Mr Archimedes, Monsieur Benedictus did not exclaim 'Eureka!' My guess is that he more probably exclaimed 'Merde!'; but when he retrieved the flask he found to his surprise that it had not shattered but had finely cracked all over retaining its shape.

On examination he found that the cellulose-acetate had formed a fine skin on the inside of the flask, which held the pieces together. This gave him furiously to think, and, in due course, he progressed to the first 'sandwich' method of coating two sheets of glass with the correct solution of cellulose-acetate, placing a sheet of celluloid between them, and compressing the sheets together.

It was roughly this method which he first patented, and sold a licence for manufacture in England to a certain Mr Reginald Delpech, who, in 1911, first registered the trade-mark 'Triplex', and floated a company called The Triplex Safety Glass Co. Ltd.

This company operated during the First World War, producing laminated glass, mainly for windshields for open cockpit aircraft, and also for pilots' goggles.

When the war ended they tried to break into the motor industry, supplying windscreens for cars. As has happened with many revolutionary innovations, the motor manufacturers were slow to accept them, and, in 1920, Triplex were almost forced out of business. They re-formed the company and struggled on until, some time in 1926, they landed a contract with the Austin Motor Company, of Longbridge Birmingham, the first motor manufacturers to fit safety-glass windscreens to production cars. Austin stipulated that Triplex should establish a factory within convenient distance of Longbridge, and a director of Austin's told them that he happened to know just the very site for them, at Kings Norton.

By an odd coincidence, the site just happened to belong to the director in question.

So the Kings Norton factory was established, and was just settling down to serious production when, in 1928, young Mr C. K. Horne arrived for his very first appointment.

He was interviewed by the Works Manager, Major Dick, who obviously knew how to pick a winner when he saw one. He enquired what degrees and other academic qualifications Kenneth had gained at Cambridge.

'None at all, I'm afraid sir,' replied Kenneth.

'How about sport?' asked the Major.

'Well, I did manage to scrape a half-blue for tennis, and I played rugger for Magdalene.'

'Splendid!' said the Major. 'We're trying to form a rugger team at the moment, and so far we've only got fourteen men. You're obviously just the man we need. Start on Monday. Thirty bob a week.'

So, like so many captains of industry before him, C. K. Horne started at the bottom of the ladder. He went into the factory, and, bit by bit, he learned about glass. He learnt how to cut it, how to polish it, and most important, how to sell it.

Major Dick and his wife took him under their wing, and invited him to live in their house for a time, until he found rooms with a Mrs Dawson, in a comfortable house in Middleton Hall Road, Kings Norton.

In the house next door lived Mr and Mrs Ernest Burgess with their twelve-year-old daughter Joan and her young brother. Ernest Burgess was Chairman and managing director of Harrison's (Birmingham) Ltd., a long established company of brassfounders.

Joan was a pretty little girl, full of gaiety and humour, and it wasn't long before she noticed the good-looking jolly young man next door who very soon became a friend of the family. One of her earliest recollections is of being taken by him with her father and mother to the Theatre Royal, Birmingham, to see Fred and Adele Astaire in that magical Gershwin musical *Funny Face*, on its pre-London tour. It was a totally enchanted evening. The very first grown-up show she had ever been to, a lovely young man, and, what is more, she was herself a passionately keen tap-dancer, so Mr Astaire's impact must have been considerable.

After this, Kenneth visited the Burgesses quite often. Joan usually opened the door to him, and he never failed to execute an intricate tap-routine on the door-step before entering the house.

Later that year, Joan went away to boarding-school at Cheltenham Ladies College, and consequently saw less of him.

The following year Kenneth moved to a flat in Sherlock Street, Kings Norton, which he shared with a colleague in the company, a young man named Hugh Borley, son of a prosperous farmer in Dorset. Hugh and Kenneth remained friends for many years.

From the very early days of the Triplex Company at Kings Norton, they seem to have established a paternalistic attitude, and to have been one big happy family. They formed a well organized Works Social and Athletic Association, which provided facilities for every kind of sport and recreation, and in which Kenneth took an active interest, serving on the committee, and later holding the office of Chairman.

Among the many games he played there, was cricket. I doubt that he was exactly a classic stylist as a batsman, but his height, powerful physique, and perfect eye made him a tremendous hitter.

In 1931 the Triplex Club was playing a match against Small Heath, on a ground surrounded by houses with nice gardens. Kenneth went in to bat, and really found his form. In one over he hit three sixes, clean out of the ground into the bordering gardens, where the balls were never seen again. As the third replacement ball was tossed out from the pavilion, the Small Heath captain approached Kenneth at the batting crease.

'Ay, lad,' he said, 'ease oop a bit. That's t'last ball we've got. If y'lose that we'll 'ave t'pack oop!'

He was, of course, a natural choice for the announcer at the Association's annual fetes, and his colleagues can claim the distinction of having heard his very earliest ever 'broadcasts', which consisted of such immortal utterances as:

'Will the competitors for the obstacle-race please assemble at the starting-line.'

Even with that lousy script he probably managed to build it up with a few gags. He particularly excelled himself a few years later, in 1936, when the Association promoted an aerobatic display, for which he provided a brilliant running-commentary.

His earliest transport was a motor-bike and sidecar, which he had for quite a few years and was very dear to his heart if perhaps scarcely sophisticated enough for his image.

Kenneth looked around for ways of augmenting his slender income, and opened a small shop, in The Cotteridge in Kings Norton, selling gramophone records. How he ever found time to attend to this in addition to his regular employment at Triplex, is hard to explain. He seems to have been personally in attendance to quite an extent, clearly he was the main attraction, and the girls came from far and wide (sometimes even *buying records!*). It was not long before his masters at Triplex frowned on this venture, and persuaded him to abandon it. They took a kindlier view of his next enterprise, when he teamed up with a kindred spirit at the works named Norman Aylward, always known as 'Bo', and formed a dance band. An interest which he had developed at Cambridge was learning to play the clarinet; and with a certain amount of help and encouragement from Harry Roy, a prominent band-leader of the twenties, he had become quite good at it.

Another illustrious contemporary of his at Cambridge was a young South American named Fred Elizalde; a name which, I am sure, is revered even today among the earlier generation of jazz buffs! Elizalde was one of the most sensationally brilliant jazz pianists I ever heard. I had the good fortune to meet him in 1927, and to stand at the side of the keyboard while he played. When I went home in the early hours of the morning I almost decided to give up piano playing for evermore.

'Bo' Aylward played the alto saxophone, and had in tow a pianist and a drummer, so he suggested that Ken would be most valuable on tenor sax, presumably doubling on clarinet. I don't know quite what he used for money, but he went straight out and bought a tenor saxophone, and persuaded Bo to give him lessons on it. Ken's enthusiasm was boundless, and he made a certain amount of progress, in the course of which he also made some pretty hideous noises, usually rather late at night in the Aylward household, where the lessons took place.

Eventually the group got going, under the title of 'Bo Aylward and His Rascals'. They played 'gigs' in

Coventry, Oxford, Warwick and Church Stretton ('local boy makes good!'), and also of course in the Triplex Social Club. Later, resplendent in faultless tails, Ken fronted the band with his saxophone, trying (as he said) 'to pretend I was an expert, without destroying the illusion by actually blowing!' He also sang 'in a glorious voice' the vocals through a megaphone (it was pre-microphone days), 'to the amazement of the dancers', though Bo Aylward maintained that the vocals were the hit of the group.

He always had a passionate attachment to his saxophone, which continued all through his life. He kept it wrapped in a pair of long red-flannel drawers, with which he lovingly polished it. I never found out where they came from.

One of his contemporaries at Magdalene had been Henry Pelham-Clinton-Hope, eldest son and heir of the eighth Duke of Newcastle, with whom he was very friendly. The Duke and his family lived at that time at Dorking, in Surrey, where Kenneth was invited to stay.

Here he met the youngest daughter, Lady Mary, then barely seventeen, with whom he formed an immediate and very strong friendship. Mary, something of a tomboy character, had an enthusiasm for cars, and driving them. She had first learnt to drive at the tender age of fourteen, on the ducal estate at Clumber, in Nottinghamshire, where she badgered her father into allowing her to be taught by the chauffeur. The Duke later bought her a second-hand Essex two-seater, with the promise that if she managed to keep it undamaged for one year, and achieve a standard of reasonable proficiency in driving, he would give her a new car. Shortly before her seventeenth birthday she proudly showed her father the Essex, still unscathed, and, true to his bargain, he said she could have her new car. She chose a Rover eight horse-power (a car I well remember having coveted at that time!) and a few weeks later (lying about her age), she got her first driving licence.

The following year Mary and her brother were invited to The White House for a tennis weekend with the Hornes. By now, of course, Kenneth was an executive of the Triplex Glass Company. He duly admired Mary's car, but was quick to point out that it lacked one refinement. It was *not* fitted with Triplex Safety Glass! Here was something which he was in a position to remedy, and he suggested that they should drive the car to Kings Norton on the Monday where he would use his influence to have this deficiency remedied.

They started off on the journey in the pouring rain, with Mary at the wheel, and halfway there, driving along a narrow country road, a cow suddenly ran headlong out of a gateway across the front of the car. Mary, faced with the alternative of the cow or a brick wall, chose the cow. It escaped undamaged, which was more than could be said for the front of the car. With roadside repairs, they were able to complete the journey to Kings Norton. Here, Kenneth, pulling out all the stops, persuaded his chums not only to fit the safety glass, but also to repair the damage, and he restored the cherished Rover, good as new, to his love, which undoubtedly sent his stock soaring.

Their friendship grew and blossomed. Sometime within the next two years they became officially engaged.

CUT GLASS

The Duke clearly adored his youngest daughter. Mary was headstrong and used to getting her own way. She and her father, affectionately known as 'the old man', 'fought like cat and dog'. 'The old man' was quite amiably disposed to her 'young man', though, surprisingly, Kenneth was terrified of him. It was a fine old emotional mish-mash all round!

Mary's elder sister, Doria, was then married; so too was Pelham. Mary clearly was determined not to be left out. 'The old man' tried to reason with her. His Grace and The Honourable Mrs Katharine Horne even met to discuss the situation over luncheon. But it was all quite pointless, as they might have known.

So, in September 1930, 'a marriage was arranged' and quietly took place, quite inexplicably at Hampstead Church; with His Grace giving the bride away. Mary was twenty, Kenneth twenty-three.

They honeymooned in Dinard, and returned to what Mary called 'a furnished semi-detached in Solihull'; perhaps a determined attempt by Kenneth to stand on his own feet.

Little Lady Mary Horne did not take kindly to domestic life. It bored her to distraction. She filled her days by visiting every cinema in Birmingham. By now the Rover had been traded for a smart Hudson coupé, and she had this to play with. Kenneth had not then progressed beyond the motor-bike and sidecar; and, what is more, used to take her out in it, and taught her to ride it. She didn't take to it instinctively, and, in the course of one of her lessons (with Ken in the sidecar) drove it at a brisk speed through a twelve-inch-deep ford, which discouraged further lessons!

CUT GLASS

After the first year, they bought a house further out in Solihull, which was made possible by Mary's trustees. They furnished it together, shopping in Birmingham. This provided a slight diversion, but neither of them could be described as a natural home maker.

Some weekends were spent with 'the old man' at Dorking, some with Mrs Horne. They travelled down in the Hudson, which only Mary drove. With most of the family now dispersed, The White House had been sold, and Mrs Horne had bought a house in Campden Hill Gardens, W.8, where she lived with her unmarried children.

There was a Horne family reunion at Christmas, which Kenneth and Mary attended, and the traditional Christmas Show was presented, still with Kenneth helping to write and produce the material, and Mary being persuaded to take part.

They seem to have been comparatively happy for the first year of the marriage; it is doubtful if they were ever passionately in love, though they always had a close and loving friendship. Sadly, there was some physical incompatibility, which was apparently irreconcilable. Probably from frustration and boredom, Mary wrote of it to her father.

The Duke's reply arrived on the breakfast table two days later.

'The old man wants me to go home at the weekend, —alone.'

'Oh! Then you'd better go. I don't want to come.'

'I could drop you off at Campden Hill.'

'All right.'

She dropped him off and drove on to Dorking. Inside the house he found a letter from the Duke. It told him Mary was not coming back to him.

It was a bitter shock. He tried to telephone her. All his calls were intercepted. Mary was forbidden to answer the telephone. She was kept a virtual prisoner at Dorking.

Kenneth did not make any effort to see the Duke, or persuade Mary to return; which may seem, at best, faint-hearted, if not pusillanimous, but who can say? This is a part of his life which remains shrouded in mystery, and it is difficult to assess his true reaction to this unhappy event.

Within the year, at the Duke's instigation, Mary was granted 'an annulment of the marriage on her own petition.'

Poor little rich girl!

Kenneth realized that work was a serious necessity, and he worked hard, because he wanted to get on. He also continued to play hard, because sport was a driving force in his life for which he had a tremendous enjoyment. In addition to his activities with the Triplex Social and Athletic Association, he also played rugger for Kings Norton in the seven-a-side league for quite a few years, and squash, at which he won the Championship of Worcestershire.

There was one certain lady for whom he had a deep affection at this time, and who indeed was devoted to him. She was happily and fairly recently married, and reluctant to jeopardize her marriage. So there was no affair as such, which, with hindsight, she regrets.

They remained 'good friends'.

4 the girl next door

In 1933, in Joan's last term at Cheltenham Ladies College, her mother sent her a cutting from a Birmingham newspaper announcing the break-up of Kenneth's marriage to Mary. On the bottom of the cutting she had written: 'A chance for me yet!'

Joan left school, and an indulgent Daddy presented her, for Christmas, with a dashing little motor-car, the very newest model Austin 10 'Swallow' drophead coupé, painted pale green.

The Burgesses had now moved farther out to a pretty house with a large garden called The Dell, at Northfield.

The car was Joan's pride and joy; she drove it everywhere. Coming into Kings Norton one day, she saw approaching her another Austin 'Swallow' identical to her own, except that it was pale blue. It drew up rather suddenly, and out of it, with a dramatic sweep and a low bow, stepped Kenneth Horne. He was astounded. Was this really the girl next door from Middleton Hall Road, who only six years earlier he used to treat like a kid sister? She was no kid sister now. Eighteen years old, a tiny little blonde, and

radiantly pretty! The twin cars made a splendid
starting point. She took him home to Northfield.
Daddy and Mummy were delighted; they had always
been fond of him. I think he fell in love with her that
day. It was not long before she adored him. They had
a wealth of interests in common. Joan was a first class
squash player, also playing for the county. She played
tennis and golf; they went dancing. It was—'just one
of those things'.

On September 5th, 1936, one month before Joan's
twenty-first birthday, they were married, with a full-
scale white wedding, and a big reception at The Dell.
Hugh Borley gave them, for a wedding present, a
golden cocker spaniel puppy, which they christened
'Snip'. They were devoted to him. Apart from his
childhood, it was the only dog Kenneth ever had.

They went for their honeymoon to Jersey, where
they stayed in splendour at The Palace Hotel, before
settling down to married life in a pretty house called
White Lodge, 'almost in the country', at Burcot.

November was a busy time for Kenneth, when he
went to London for the whole period of the Motor
Show, then held at Olympia, where Triplex of course
had a stand.

One afternoon he was leaving the main hall, going
into the entrance area through a pair of heavy swing-
doors. As he pushed on the door to go out, someone
pushed on it to go in. Kenneth won from his side, and
as the door opened who should he find on the other side
but Mary.

'Hello! What are you doing here?'

'I'm supposed to meet some friends to go to the

show. They're half-an-hour late already.'

'Well, come and have some tea.'

'What about my friends?'

'Oh, you'll find them!'

They had tea, in the course of which he asked:

'What are you doing tonight? Come out to dinner.'

She looked at him in amazement. 'How about your wife?'

'Oh, she isn't coming up until tomorrow.'

She burst out laughing. 'You never change, do you. How long have you been married?'

'Let me see. It's just—six weeks now.'

Kenneth and Joan joined the Barnt Green Sports and Social Club and soon became its leading lights. Joan, still mad for tap-dancing, appeared at a Club dance in the cabaret, with a number in which she was dressed as Minnie Mouse, and had a dummy Mickie Mouse, with which she danced. It was the hit of the evening, and they asked her to repeat it at the next dance. This time she had another idea. She made a special Micky Mouse costume for Ken, who danced the number with her as a huge Micky with a miniscule Minnie!

As a complete reversal from his first marriage, Kenneth became very domesticated. They entertained quite a lot, and it was Kenneth who fixed the snacks for cocktail parties. He also actually made for her a triple mirror, which delighted his friends, who had never before known him to knock in a nail.

Almost at once, Joan became pregnant, and their cup of happiness was complete. On July 21st, 1937, she gave birth to a son. He was stillborn.

THE GIRL
NEXT DOOR

It was a bitter tragedy for these two happy people. The bottom dropped out of their world. Kenneth was infinitely loving and comforting, making every possible effort for Joan.

As soon as she was well enough, he arranged a holiday. They took the car to Germany, and drove gently through the Black Forest. They stayed away for three weeks, no expense spared. By the time they came home, and Ken was faced with the expenses of Joan's confinement, he was rather strapped for money. Things had improved a bit since the legendary thirty-bob-a-week days, but he always had rather expensive tastes, and was trying to dream up ways of producing that little bit extra.

Which may explain why, some time the following year, in the course of a drink with a friend named Edmund King, a young chartered accountant who worked in Birmingham, Ken said:

'Got any money?'

'No,' replied Edmund.

'Neither have I. But I've got a red hot tip, and I think we can make some. I've heard that Triplex are going to lose the Austin contract, and a firm called Lancegay Glass are going to get it. This news will break at the next Austin board-meeting in a couple of weeks. Now, Lancegay shares at present are about sixpence, but when the news of the contract breaks they're bound to rocket. If we buy them at a tanner, we can sell before the end of the account and make a nice little profit.'

'Great!' said Edmund. 'Leave it to me. I've got a pal who's a broker in Birmingham, I'll do it through him.'

They had another drink on the strength of it. They

were clearly on the way to that 'first million'.

A few days later, on the telephone:

'Ken? Edmund. I've bought ten thousand at six-and-a-quarter. Looks as though they're moving already. Keep it dark, eh?'

They waited.

One week later. Hitler invades Austria. The Stock Market, with its customary hysteria, slumps sharply. Lancegay drop to fourpence.

Two weeks later. The board meeting of the Austin Motor Company. The Triplex contract is *renewed*. Lancegay shares drop to threepence.

Three weeks later. Account day; and, even having cut their losses, the boys get a bill from the broker which shows them a loss on the deal of one hundred and twenty-seven pounds!

Four weeks later. Triplex take-over Lancegay!

They met, for another drink. (Probably, a half of bitter!) It was a fortune, and they just hadn't got it. Edmund went to see his pal the broker, who was sympathetic and as helpful as possible. But it took them the best part of a year before they cleared that debt.

It's called 'learning the hard way'!

5 "per ardua..."

IT would probably be fanciful to suggest that this little debacle left Kenneth with a personal grudge against Hitler, but it was not very long afterwards that he took himself off and enlisted in the R.A.F. Volunteer Reserve, on a part-time training scheme. He was granted a commission as Acting Pilot-Officer and posted to 911 Squadron (Barrage Balloons), attached to No. 5 Centre at Sutton Coldfield.

The training was spasmodic, as there wasn't much equipment and only one balloon, but there seems to have been a great deal of goodwill among the personnel. Kenneth, with his flair for organization, quickly got some entertainments going, in which he himself took an active part, singing comic songs and playing the saxophone.

When war was declared, Joan and Kenneth left their house at Burcot, and stored their furniture. The Burgesses had moved from Northfield back to Edgbaston, which was fortuitous for Kenneth, since A. Flight Headquarters, to which he was now attached, was just there, and he and Joan were able to live with them.

Joan now became a camp-follower for the next two years.

Kenneth was given the exalted title of Flight-Commander, with his very own balloon named Agnes, which was flown from a site just off the Wolverhampton Road.

Barrage balloons, it seems, were fairly temperamental, and inclined, not infrequently, to leak, which caused them to lose height and career drunkenly across the sky. Agnes's cable once became entangled with a factory chimney, and neatly sliced the top off it.

Among the 'other ranks' at No. 5 Centre, had been a young man who (in the strictest sense of the phrase) was later to make a name for himself; and, without further explanation at the moment, let me say that his name was Edward Wilkinson. He had not been commissioned by the time that he too was posted to A. Flight H.Q. under the command of Pilot-Officer Horne. Equipment was still in very short supply, and personnel were encouraged to use their own transport for service duties.

Aircraftsman Wilkinson was appointed driver to the Flight-Commander. He was never quite sure why, unless it had something to do with the fact that he happened to own a Jaguar. He also, conveniently, happened to own a flat in the vicinity, where some excellent parties were staged, and democracy was not unduly strained on either side when Pilot-Officer Horne and Aircraftsman Wilkinson became very good friends.

Kenneth was always an enthusiastic cook, and in 1939

he was responsible for some 'sumptuous repasts' at these parties. Meat was a bit of a problem, but they found a tame butcher, Len Houghton, in Broad Street, Birmingham, with a shop conveniently opposite 'The Crown'. They would drop into the shop for a friendly chat with Len, and invite him across to 'The Crown', where their hospitality became lavish. They would then see Len safely back to the shop, where quite often he would fling open the door of his freezer-room and say: 'Help yer bloody selves!'

This was the time of the Phoney War, when the worst enemy was boredom. Kenneth formed a concert party from the available talent, and, from all reports, the talent was of a very high standard. He wrote special topical sketches and material, and compered the show himself. Joan, with her tap-dance routines, contributed valuably to the success of the show.

Edward distinguished himself as a volunteer strip-tease artist, supposedly standing in for one who had failed to turn up. He peeled off his clothes to suitable music, until he was left in a pair of woollen combinations with an L-plate on his behind. The whole glorious production was staged at The Talbot Hotel at Oldbury, where it was a riotous success.

B.B.C. producer Bill McClurg, then at Birmingham, saw the show and immediately engaged them to take part in a programme he was producing called 'Ack-Ack Beer-Beer', which was the particular service jargon for Anti-Aircraft Balloon Barrage. Kenneth compered the show, which was duly transmitted from the Birmingham station of the B.B.C., without anyone realizing what an historic broadcast it was to turn out to be.

In September 1939, Kenneth had met up with Edmund King again, and talked him into joining the R.A.F.V.R. Edmund was also taken into Balloon Barrage, but was sent to a unit in Smethwick.

By early 1940, the No. 5 Centre crowd seemed to drift apart. Edward Wilkinson got his commission and was posted to Liverpool. He didn't see Ken again during the war, but shortly afterwards he was boarding a train at Manchester station and hoisting his luggage on to the rack when a fruity voice behind him said:

'I'm afraid, sir, you will have to get out of this carriage; it is reserved for women only!'

It was a great reunion.

In August 1940, he had a short posting, as Acting Squadron-Leader, to 966 Squadron at Newport, Monmouthshire, on an administration course. Old faithful camp-follower tagged along. They arrived to find that they had been allotted a married-quarter house on the base, and a full-time batman, which was high living.

The following April saw him back in Birmingham for six months, and in November 1941 his rank was confirmed and he was posted to No. 32 Group H.Q. at a large country house called Claverton Manor near Bath. It could have been a coincidence that a few months later Squadron-Leader Edmund King was posted to the same station.

Joan went with him, and they lived out in a beautiful house almost opposite the station. Some time during the summer of 1942, they went out for dinner at The Swan Hotel at Bradford-on-Avon. At a table across the room was a party of W.A.A.F. officers. Joan was rather silent for a while, then she said:

'What on earth am I doing here? I ought to be doing something. I think I'm going to join the W.A.A.F.'

Kenneth did not immediately reply, but after a moment he said: 'Yes. I think that would be very good.'

This was clearly a turning point in what, up till then, had been a happy and successful marriage for more than five years; but did Kenneth have any premonition at all?

Joan had a close school-friend named Valerie St Ludger, whose family also lived near Birmingham. Val was already in the First Aid Nursing Yeomanry, stationed in Wiltshire, and not particularly happy.

Joan telephoned her the next day.

'Val, do you think you could get out of those old FANY's? I want to join the W.A.A.F. Will you come with me?'

Val agreed. Next, Joan telephoned her parents with her big decision. Her mother was dismayed, and rather unhappy. There was really no reason. It was a splendid decision of Joan's. And yet, looking back, it was almost as though her mother had some sort of premonition about it perhaps not being such a good thing. She adored her daughter, and could not really find an argument against her. Within the next few days, Val and Joan got on the train and went to Birmingham. All the parents met them at the station; took them to the Grand Hotel and socked them a splendid but rather uneasy lunch. The following day, the girls drove in Joan's car to R.A.F. Bridgnorth, in Shropshire, where they had been directed. They arrived at the gate and reported to the duty Corporal.

'We've come to enlist,' announced Joan.

'Oh yes?' said the Corporal.

There was a pause. Several 'erks' in the vicinity gathered round, eyeing these two dishy dollies hopefully.

'What shall we do with the car?' asked Joan.

A great guffaw went up. Then:

'Ao! *What* shall we *do* with the *corr*?' chorused the group.

It was their baptism by fire!

Within days, poor Val was stricken down with mumps. So Joan's lovely plan of having her friend to support her went sadly awry.

She was enlisted, and very soon posted to a station at Colerne, near Bath. As an Airwoman she was not permitted to live out, but at least she was able to see Kenneth whenever possible. As soon as she could, she applied for a commission, selecting 'Operations' as her first choice. The best she managed to achieve, however, was 'Administration', which was comparatively dull. In due time, she was sent to Windermere on her commission course. It was their first real separation. However, her first posting as an officer, turned out to be to Fighter Command, at Rudlow Manor, near Bath, and she was able to be billeted with Kenneth again at the nearby village of Corsham.

Kenneth's designation was Squadron-Leader P.1, and he was responsible for dealing with the legal aspects of service life, courts martial, courts of enquiry etc.

He once had to hold a court of enquiry into a complaint by a local farmer that airmen had left open a gate on his land, allowing a valuable horse to escape. The horse had slipped on the tarmac, injuring its leg, for which the owner was claiming what seemed to be exorbitant damages. At the end of the proceedings, Kenneth prepared an official report of the findings for the A.O.C., in which he dealt seriously with every aspect of the case. The report concluded:

'I have called on Mr J— personally, and expressed regret for the accident, but I was unable to persuade him to reduce his claim. Judging by the value he puts upon his horse, I can only assume that it is the original Weston super mare.'

As a part of his general duties on the station, he of course served his turns as Orderly Officer, and in this capacity he was required to visit the Mess Hall with his accompanying N.C.O to oversee the meal of the other ranks.

'The Orderly Officer would normally wear his hat, as he was on duty, but Squadron-Leader Horne, on entering the Mess Hall, would remove his and carry it. He said he wouldn't like anyone to walk through his dining-room with their hat on, so he wasn't going to do so.'

Another of his duties as Orderly Officer was a periodical inspection of the fire-escape arrangements. There was a large contingent of W.A.A.F.s at Claverton Manor, who occupied the top floor of the mansion. One of their fire-escapes was a fixed metal ladder which led from outside a bathroom window down to the roof of the dining-hall and thence to the ground. On the day of his inspection, Kenneth always made a point of telephoning the W.A.A.F. Duty Officer to advise her of his visit, and to say that in the course of it he and his N.C.O. would be climbing the metal ladder. On one occasion the message was not passed on. Kenneth mounted the ladder and flung open the bathroom window. There was a shrill squawk as he beheld a totally naked W.A.A.F. about to enter her bath. It was the only time the Squadron-Leader was ever seen off balance.

Kenneth, recounting the story in the Officers' Mess that night, said: 'She was a very smart girl, you know, she just grabbed a sponge and covered her face!'

Edmund King arrived at Claverton Manor, where, to his delight, he found he was to share an office with Kenneth. The third member of the office was a Flight-Lieutenant Bazely, and, half way through the first morning, Kenneth looked up from his work and said:

'Bazely, don't you think it's about time you got out Squadron-Leader King's file?'

Bazely looked at his watch.

'Of course, sir. It *is* half past eleven. Right away!'

He crossed to a filing cabinet and pulled out the bottom drawer. It was packed with bottles of beer!

Edmund remembers 1942 as the happiest year of his war, and Kenneth as the most popular man on the station. Everybody loved him, from the officers to other ranks, of both sexes. The only dissentient voice was the C.O., an ex-regular army major, who then held the exalted rank of Air-Commodore. He was a small man, with an inverse ratio of pomposity, which so often seems to happen. His officers were always icily polite to

47

him in the Mess, but he was not the most popular character.

Early in 1943, Kenneth was posted again, this time to Air Ministry, in London, with promotion to Wing-Commander. Claverton Manor was sad to see him go, but quite shortly afterwards he had occasion to revisit the station, and they threw a party for him in the Mess. He arrived a few minutes late, and all the officers, including the C.O., were already assembled in the bar.

Ken made one of his celebrated entrances, beaming all over his face, and was greeted with warm cries of welcome. He advanced, smiling, upon the C.O. with arms outstretched.

'Why, *sir*!' he cried. 'How simply *splendid* to see you again!' He then picked up the C.O. by the waist, put him across his shoulder and waltzed him round the bar. There was a fraction of a second's incredulous silence. Then the bar exploded in howls of laughter. The unfortunate Air-Commodore was restored to his feet, purple in the face, but realizing there was really nothing he could do about it. After all, Wing-Commander Horne was a guest of the Mess!

His first duty on arrival at Air Ministry, was as assistant to a certain Wing-Commander Christian Stock, who had also previously been at Claverton Manor. One morning Kenneth's telephone rang, and someone from that station asked to speak to Wing-Commander Stock. Kenneth replied:

'Sorry, Christian's away. Salute the happy Horne!'

6 "...ad astra"

KENNETH's posting to Air Ministry in London, in 1943, was an event of great significance, when one remembers that this was really the first time he had ever lived and worked there in his adult life. He took a small flat at Kensington Close, where Joan was able to spend her leaves with him.

His early broadcasts in 'Ack-Ack Beer-Beer' had not gone unrecognized, and now that he was in London he got himself, in his spare time, into some shows for a war-time organization called Overseas Recorded Broadcasting Service (ORBS for short), which made recorded programmes for transmission to the Services in the Middle East. In these shows he acted as compere and general announcer, and on one of them he met for the first time a certain Flight-Lieutenant Richard Murdoch, who, he was well aware, was already an established broadcaster. Dickie Murdoch was doing an act on his own in the show, and, to introduce him, Kenneth said:

'And now that you are round your radio-sets, let's go over again to that well-remembered R.A.F. station, which tonight comes off the secret list again, Much-

Binding-in-the-Marsh. And waiting at the gate to welcome you is its Station Commander, Flight-Lieutenant Richard Murdoch.'

That was the first time Dickie had ever heard of Much-Binding-in-the Marsh. He didn't know then how many times he was to hear about it again!

After the programme, they lunched together, and discovered they had a lot in common, including the fact that Dick had been a contemporary of Kenneth's at Cambridge (at Pembroke College) though they had never met. Kenneth asked if Dickie was happy in his work. Dickie replied: 'No, not particularly.' Kenneth said: 'Well, there's a Squadron-Leader's post in my department going spare. Would you like it?' And that was the start of a great friendship and a radio partnership which lasted over the next twelve years.

The department of Air Ministry in which they worked was known as War Organization, and their section dealt with the supply of aircraft to Russia. They shared an office, Kenneth claimed: 'working jolly hard', and who shall doubt him. They seem to have been involved in a lot of liaison work with Russian Supply Missions, and the hospitality of their gallant allies called for a lot of stamina. After one particularly heavy lunchtime conference, Kenneth, dozing gently in his office, was woken by the telephone ringing. As he lifted it from the cradle, an urgent voice said:

'What about those tanks for Russia?'

Without a moment's hesitation, Kenneth replied: 'Do nothing till you hear from me,' and hung up.

But, whether in or out of the office, Dickie, an experienced professional actor for some twelve years, recognized instantly that Kenneth was an absolute natural as a comedian, and quickly set about organizing this budding career. He first talked to Harry S. Pepper, the producer of 'Monday Night at Eight', in which he was then appearing, and got Ken into the show. His early broadcasts were as chairman of a quiz in the programme called 'Puzzle Corner'.

I don't know how many of these programmes he took part in, but clearly ideas were now sparking around like fireworks, and it was not long before a pattern began to take shape. Dickie felt that there was a wealth of untapped material in Ken's idea of that remote Air Force station somewhere in Britain called 'Much-Binding-in-the-Marsh', and together they developed it.

Kay Bagley, a former Flight-Officer in the W.A.A.F., had been with Kenneth at Claverton Manor, and followed him to Air Ministry, where she occupied the next-door office. She and her colleagues were the 'dog' on which the earlier 'Much-Binding' gags were tried with the ink scarcely dry.

'Ken was a marvellous person to have as a friend, and any of us who felt depressed or fed-up agreed that ten minutes with Ken was better than a tonic. In that rich fruity voice of his he would make the dullest routine matter sound funny.'

During the V-Bombs, Ken and Dickie were sleeping at the Air Ministry, which adjoined the Ministry of Health building in Whitehall. They had been out together for the evening, returning late and fairly happy. They entered by the Ministry of Health door, took a wrong turning, and found themselves in a strange office. On the desk was an in-tray full of assorted files.

The opportunity was too good to miss. They sat down at the desk, and minuted the files to various departments, writing on the minute-forms such comments as:

'Kindly let me have your views on Enclosure 2A.'

'Surely this matter should immediately be referred to QM/AG/24?'

The next morning, full of remorse, they felt they should at least call on the occupant of the office and apologize. But neither of them could remember which room they had entered or how they had reached it.

In 1944, at the R.A.F. station at Boscombe Down on Salisbury Plain, there was a rather disconsolate and desperate W.A.A.F, No. 463232 L.A.C.W. Constance Weston. She had applied two years earlier for a commission in Administration, and she hadn't even made the Selection Board. Finally, her C.O. took pity on her and suggested that she might do better to try for her commission in the Accounts Section. This struck terror into poor Connie's heart, but there seemed no way out, and she agreed.

She duly received orders to attend a Selection Board at Air Ministry in London on a given date, and as the fateful day loomed nearer she grew more and more depressed.

Passing the station notice-board she glanced up at the latest posting of Air Ministry Orders, and observed that a new commission had just been opened, under the slightly fanciful title of 'Celestial Navigation', for which applications from W.A.A.F. officer-cadets were invited. It seemed to have something to do with teaching air-crew to fly. The details of the scheme were somewhat nebulous, but Connie seemed to have the necessary qualifications at least to apply, and anything would be better than working in Accounts.

She travelled to London, and presented herself to her Selection Board, where, taking her courage in both hands, she spoke up, and told this august assembly of high-ranking officers that she didn't *really* feel her heart was in becoming an Accounts officer, but might it perhaps be possible for her to apply for Celestial Navigation?

There was an uneasy pause, then:

'Celestial Navigation,' said the Chairman ruminatively.

'H'm. What do you think about that, Wing-Commander?'

'*Well*, sir,' said the wing-commander ponderously, 'of course it is a very new commission. Would the applicant have the necessary qualifications?'

'Ye-es, that's the question, of course. Well—er—Weston, I really think you would have a better chance in Accounts. In fact I think we would be prepared to sanction your application for that. But, Celestial Navigation? I'm not so sure.'

'Could I have permission just to apply, sir?'

'Well, I tell you what,' said the Chairman. 'We'll give you one week to find someone to recommend you for this—er—, for this—er—other commission. But if you can't do that, you'll have to go to Accounts. Is that clear?'

L.A.C.W. Weston dismissed smartly, feeling fairly depressed. She got a fresh 'Application for Commission' form, and completed the details. She then prowled the Air Ministry corridors for hours making enquiries at

various offices. No one had even heard of Celestial
Navigation. Finally, one more sympathetic character
with a cryptic smile suggested she might try Room 200,
to which he directed her. On the door were two names:
WING-COMMANDER C. K. HORNE. SQUADRON-LEADER R.
MURDOCH.

She knocked, and a deep voice invited her to enter.
Standing at a desk, was a tall dark balding figure;
behind him a somewhat slighter character with fair
hair.

L.A.C.W. Weston stood to attention.

'Excuse me, sir. I'm trying to find somebody who
might be able to give me some information about
Celestial Navigation, and I wondered if you could help
me, sir.'

A ghost of a smile flickered across the wing-commander's face.

'Ah, yes. Celestial Navigation,' he said. 'Well, what
exactly do you want to know?'

'Well, sir. I'd like to apply for a commission, sir.
I've just attended a Board for a commission in
Accounts, and—I don't think I could *bear* Accounts,
sir, and they said that if I could get somebody to recommend me for Celestial Navigation, sir, I needn't take
the other commission, sir.'

'I *see*,' said the Wing-Commander. 'Well, I think
she'd do, don't you, Murdoch?'

The Squadron-Leader, with serious concentration,
inspected her for a moment.

'Oh, absolutely, sir. Just the type they're looking for,
I'm sure.'

'Right, then!' said the wing-commander. 'Let's have

1. The Horne Family, Ampthill Square, 1908. (*Left to right*) Joan, Ronald, Oliver, Bridget and Dorothy. (*In front*) Ruth and a strapping Charles Kenneth aged 18 months, sits beside Dorothy.

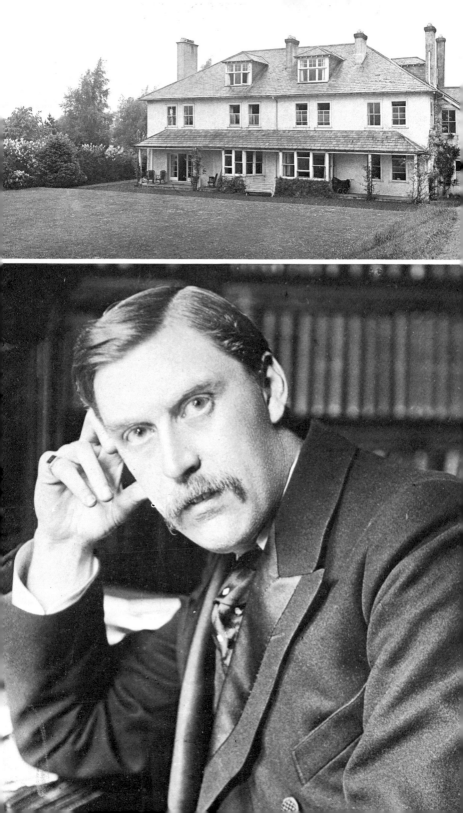

(*Opposite top*) The White House,
Church Stretton.
(*Opposite below*) The Rev. Charles
Silvester Horne.

(*Right*) Kenneth, 1920.

(*Below*) The Hon. Mrs. Katharine
Horne.

6. (*Opposite*) Uncle
Austin Pilkington.

7. The Right Honourable
Lord Cozens-Hardy,
Q.C., M.P. (later Lord
Cozens-Hardy, Master of
The Rolls), a cartoon by
Spy, dated April 13th,
1898.

8. Cambridge University Lawn Tennis team, Germany, 1926. (*Back*) Russell Young, Kenneth Horne; (*front*) H. W. ("Bunny") Austin, Bill Powell, Jackie Baines.

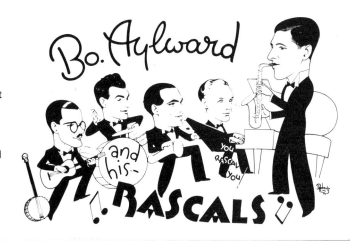

9. (*Opposite*) The Obst Club. Bunny Austin, Kenneth Horne, Russell Young.

10. (*Right*) Bo Aylward and his Rascals.

11. (*Below*) Kenneth ("Curly") Horne, 1928.

A victim's impression of MR C.K. HORNE

CAMARAD

12. (*Left*) Demon Horne, at Wimbledon.
13. (*Below*) Mr. Kenneth and Lady Mary Horne, 1930.

14. (*Opposite top*) The Austin Swallow coupé, 1935.
15. (*Opposite below*) Mr. and Mrs. Kenneth Horne (Joan) with Snip, 1936

"MUCH-BINDING-IN-
THE-MARSH"

16. (*Opposite top*) "Oh Sir,
it *is* good to see you!"

17. (*Opposite below*)
"When I was in Sidi
Barrani . . ."

18. (*Above*) Flight-Officer
Flannel (Maureen Riscoe)
meets Dudley Davenport
(Maurice Denham),
Murdoch, Sir and Costa.

19. (*Left*) Sound effects :
"Miranda" the mermaid
(Glynis Johns) prepares to
dive, assisted by Murdoch,
Sir and Costa.

0. (*Opposite top*) "The Other" Kenneth Horne with K.H. and Marjorie.
1. (*Opposite below*) Mr. and Mrs. Kenneth Horne (Marjorie) 1945.

Smashing Time at Triplex !
2. (*Below*) Triplex party, 1951. (*Standing*) Sir Harry Pilkington,
Mr. Arthur Cochran ; (*sitting, left to right*) Susan, Marjorie, Kenneth,
Joyce Davis and friends.
3. (*Bottom*) K.H. demonstrates Armour-plated Security Glass.

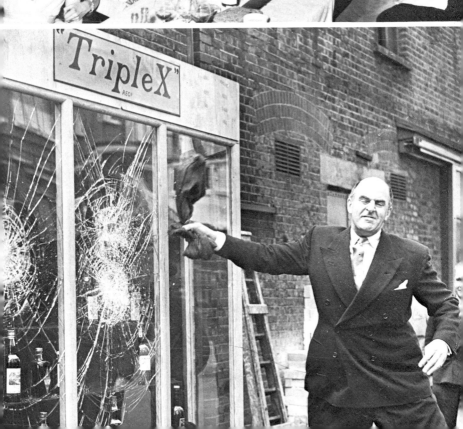

24. Susan. (*Left*) Strike-leader at St. James's.
25. (*Right*) Pastel portrait by Honor Earl, 1952.
26. (*Below*) The second Rolls, with Susan and Marjorie, 1955.

your form.' He scrawled across the form C. K. Horne. W/Cmmdr. Orgs.'

'Thank you, sir. Thank you very much, sir.'

She left the office, and returned happily to the wilds of Salisbury Plain. She dispatched the precious application form, upon which her whole future depended, and settled down to await the summons to the Celestial Navigation course.

It never came. Some months later she was commissioned, into the Intelligence Branch. Some time after that she heard that there had been another Air Ministry Order cancelling the original one asking for officer cadets to apply for Celestial Navigation. More than a year after her demobilization, she read a newspaper article about Horne and Murdoch's hoax. How they had initiated the whole idea, and passed it to another department, never thinking it could go any further; but how, in fact, it had gone the rounds and got as far as publication in Air Ministry Orders. And also how, it seemed, *one* W.A.A.F. only had actually applied to join!

7 "a little thing that goes..."

I T wouldn't have needed a genius to recognize the potential of 'Much-Binding-in-the-Marsh', and Leslie Bridgemont, a B.B.C. producer to whom they first showed it, grabbed it and booked them for the next edition of a light-hearted programme he was producing called 'Merry-go-Round', which was built around the Navy one week, the Army the second, and the R.A.F. the third, in rotation.

It wasn't exactly an overnight sensation. But Bridgemont liked it enough to ask for another instalment. Bit by bit the idea caught on, and began to be talked about. It was splendidly topical; basically the story about the officer who was so dim that even the other officers noticed! And who *was* this new chap on the wireless who had suddenly appeared from nowhere?

The whole programme could be said to have been just one of those happy accidents. So many of the most successful ventures in entertainment often are. The simple recipe for success might be summed up in one short phrase: 'Meeting the right man, in the right place, at the right time.' Of the surviving members of this brilliant company, each has been generous, and

56

honest enough, to admit that he owes any success he
may personally have achieved to all the others concerned.

In 1943, there was, for example, also in the R.A.F.,
a certain Leading-Aircraftsman Sam Costa, who had
just returned from a particularly depressing ten
months posting in Iceland, and was pretty browned-off.
Sam, before the war, had been a very successful 'crooner'
(as we used to call 'em in those days!) singing with a
number of the best recording bands, such as Jack
Hylton, Lew Stone, Ambrose and many others, but
during the war, feeling that his crooning days were
numbered, he tried his hand at becoming a comic.
After he returned to England, he seized upon every
opportunity of broadcasting which came his way; not
with the idea of making any money so much as for the
glorious relief of getting away for a day's leave and a
trip to London, with a nominal subsistence allowance
of one guinea. It was on such a trip, to ORBS to take
part in a programme, that he first met Dickie Murdoch.
Dickie's 'stooge' (whoever it might have been) had
failed to turn up, and Sam talked Dickie into letting
him take the stooge part. Dickie was quite impressed,
and said he hoped that Sam would work with him again.
'You must meet a chap called Ken Horne,' he said.
'We're working on an idea for a show for the B.B.C.,
there might be something in it for you.' Sam thanked
him, and went back to duty. Some months went by. And
then, the miracle happened. Dickie rang him, and asked
him to take part in one of the early 'Much-Binding'
programmes. And so was born that inimitable character whom they named simply 'Costa', and another

historic catch-phrase came into being with his 'Good-mornin', sir. Was there something?'

'Costa' was the butt of the programme. The dope who always got it wrong, and drove his superiors mad.

In the early days of the series, he did not necessarily appear in every episode, and his position as a regular member of the cast was by no means secure.

After he had done quite a number of shows just after the war, there was one certain script in which the C.O. and the A.O.C. (Murdoch and Horne) became particularly exasperated with Costa, and Dickie had a line something like: 'This time you've gone *too far* Costa. You'll simply have to go!'

Sam got suddenly depressed about this imaginary situation. He brooded about it all the way home. He could not rid his mind of the conviction that perhaps there might be more truth in that line in the script than he cared to believe. Was it perhaps some dreadful ploy to write him out of the show? And would he just not be booked again? The following day, still worried sick, he mentioned the whole affair to some friend. This was the spark which started the forest fire! The 'friend' talked to a friend, who talked to a friend, and, two nights later, Sam opened his evening paper and found a headline which read: 'COSTA' FIRED FROM 'MUCH-BINDING'.

He was horrified. The following day more papers picked up the story, and Sam's telephone never stopped ringing. Every Light Entertainment programme on the air wanted him to join them. He was suddenly besieged with offers. And then the telephone rang again.

"A LITTLE THING
THAT GOES..."

'Sam? What the hell's going on? I've been trying to
call you for the past half-hour.'

'Oh, hallo Ken! Er—seen the papers?'

'Of course I've seen the papers. What a load of old
codswallop! Was this your idea of a publicity stunt?'

Rather abashed, Sam explained. Kenneth roared
with laughter. But then: 'My dear chap! What a silly
fellow you are! You don't think we could get along
without you, do you? I promise you you're back again
next week.'

And he was; and from then on for the next how-ever-
many years Costa never missed a show.

I have checked Air Force records to find out the
highest rank held by 'Costa' during his term of duty
at 'Much-Binding-in-the-Marsh', and I find that he
never exceeded what was known in the Service as A/C
Plonk.

His real-life counterpart claims that, for a short
period in his Service career, he attained the giddy rank
of corporal; but, in recognition of services outside the
call of duty, he was quickly demoted to Leading-Aircraftsman.

When at last his demob came, and he returned to
civilian life, he took to signing himself 'S. Costa. L.A/C
Retired'.

Sam particularly liked Ken's story of once when he
was travelling alone by train, and the only other occu-
pants of his carriage were two elderly ladies. The train
drew in to Nuneaton station. Voices from the platform
called 'Nuneaton ... Nuneaton', and then there was one
of those total silences which sometimes occur on trains
when nobody is getting off or on. In the middle of the

"A LITTLE THING
THAT GOES..."

silence one lady leaned across to the other and remarked
quietly:

'Mildred has good reason to remember Nuneaton!'

Ken no doubt spent the rest of the journey dreaming
up a lurid variety of the most appalling experiences
which had befallen poor Mildred. And in Nuneaton,
of all places!

8 "...something like this"

1944 was the testing year for 'Much-Binding', in which it served its apprenticeship at three-weekly intervals in the 'Merry-go-Round' series. By 1945 it was firmly established as a programme in its own right, and was given a thirty-nine weeks booking as a weekly show. It was a solid success, and even the coming of peace did not disturb the formula. All that happened was that 'Much-Binding' instead of being an R.A.F. station became a civil airport, and nobody really noticed the difference. We still had 'Sir', Murdoch and Costa, and various ancillary characters.

One of the most successful of these was 'Dudley Davenport', played by that brilliant actor Maurice Denham. He also played 'Mr Bobble', the compositor, type-setting the first edition of the station newspaper *The Weekly Bind*. Running out of the letter 'e', he substituted the letter 'o', which he said they could correct by 'putting a little line across it'. To Dickie's consternation, the banner read: *THE WOOKLY BIND*, of which he is referred to as 'The Oditor'. Sam's sports column, headed 'Crickot', reads: 'Aftor tho Tost match at Loods, the Onglish toam was agrood by tho soloctors at a committoo mooting'. Dickie announced: 'They'd never stand for this in Floot Stroot!', to which Kenneth replied: 'Not a word to Bossio.'

It is hard to remember that there was ever a time when Maurice was not in 'Much-Binding', but he did not in fact join it until 1947. From then on he was a fairly regular member of the cast for the rest of the run.

In 1950-51, the whole team did a series of commercial radio programmes for Mars Bars, from Radio Luxembourg. One of the fringe benefits of this lovely job was that the sponsors were lavish in their free handouts of the product; and let me remind you, in that year of what was laughingly called 'peace', sweets were still on ration. Since Dickie, Kenneth, Maurice and Sam all had young families, they must have been the most popular Dads in the business!

In November 1947 they were invited to the staff dance at Windsor Castle, from where the show was broadcast in the presence of the Queen and Princess Margaret. In the course of the party afterwards, Dickie was dancing with Princess Margaret who told him how very popular the programme was with the Royal Family, who were regular listeners to it. Dickie asked whether they might possibly consider attending a broadcast at the Paris Studio. The Princess replied that she would very much like to, and promised to try and arrange a visit. A few days later, Dickie's telephone rang, and his wife came to him and said: 'There's a lady-in-waiting at Buckingham Palace on the 'phone.' Since practically every telephone call between Dickie and Kenneth tended to begin: 'The Archbishop of Canterbury speaking', or: 'This is the Pope', Dickie snorted, picked up the receiver and announced: 'Mahatma Gandhi here. Can I help you?'

It was a lady-in-waiting at Buckingham Palace.

She said that the Queen would like to bring a party of some ten or twelve to the broadcast at The Paris on the following Tuesday. Would Mr Murdoch be kind enough to arrange it?

Dickie quickly rang Kenneth to tell him the news, and Kenneth telephoned Leslie Bridgemont at the B.B.C.

'Oh Leslie, can I have twelve extra tickets for next Tuesday's show?'

In those halcyon days, tickets for admission to shows as popular as 'Much-Binding' were rarer than gold. People waited weeks for them. Leslie Bridgemont, faced with this extraordinary request, replied: 'Don't be bloody silly, old boy, all the tickets were sent out weeks ago.'

'Oh, what a pity,' said Ken. 'I shall just have to ring the Queen back and tell her she can't come.'

The B.B.C. did their nuts! There was a red carpet at the entrance to The Paris, the staircase and the studio-stage were stiff with flowers. There was, of course, a special and detailed rehearsal before the doors were opened. At the end of this, Kenneth pacing rather nervously about the stage came across some cigarette-ends on the floor. He looked around, and saw an un-recognized figure on the other side:

'Oh, just get these fag-ends swept up, would you,' he said somewhat peremptorily.

"...SOMETHING
LIKE THIS"

It was the Deputy Director-General of the B.B.C., who, the very next week, was given a Knighthood, Ken said, because he swept up the fag-ends so well!

It was a memorable night. All twelve of the special seats were occupied, for, at the last moment, two unexpected guests joined the party—Their Royal Highnesses Princess Elizabeth and her husband The Duke of Edinburgh. It was the Princess's first appearance in public since the birth of her son, now Prince of Wales.

Dickie made the evening by adding to their signature tune at the end, the line: 'Good old Charlie!'

This must be one of the most famous, and, I have always thought, the best radio signature tunes there have ever been. It was born in the very early days of the 'Merry-go-Round' era, when one afternoon at four o'clock Kenneth said:

'Wouldn't it be a good idea if we had a song that went:

At   Much   Binding - in - the - Marsh

'Yes,' said Dickie. 'Jolly good idea.'

They dummied out a shape, to which they wrote lyrics for four verses. At six o'clock they went to the studio and got hold of Sidney Torch, who accompanied the programme on the Hammond organ. They hummed the dummy tune and Sidney knocked it into musical shape and scribbled a top-line. At seven o'clock they broadcast it for the very first time, and from then on they used it in every programme. Over the years, they wrote more than five hundred verses for it.

On one occasion, in the middle of a broadcast, they discovered they had only written three verses instead of the usual four. Panic! They waited until the spot in the programme when Stanley Black and the orchestra played a musical number, lasting, I should imagine, no more than three minutes. They dashed into a huddle in the corner of the studio, and by the time the band number was over the fourth verse was scribbled on the back of the script. Ten minutes later they were singing it!

There were times, of course, when those seemingly effortless rhymes just wouldn't come right. Dickie remembers a 'despair' verse they wrote, which at least made *them* laugh:

'At Much-Binding-in-the-Marsh,
We're very keen on higher education,
At Much-Binding-in-the-Marsh,
We always try to learn something that's useful.
We're very keen on languages, we often study
  Greek,
Experiments in science keep us busy every day,
And when we're in despair we often make up
  rhymes like this,
At Much-Binding-in-the-Marsh.'

Then there was the wartime one, the middle of which went:

'To camouflage the aeroplane, instead of using
  net,

"...SOMETHING
LIKE THIS"

The other day we painted it, but much to our
  regret,
We did it so successfully we haven't found it yet
At Much-Binding-in-the-Marsh.'

They appeared at the very first Royal Command
Variety Broadcast, which took place in the Concert
Hall, at Broadcasting House, on Kenneth's birthday,
February 27th, 1953. This was Coronation Year, and
of course there had to be a very special verse to round
off the act.

The special words of 'the little thing that goes something like this' were:

'At Much-Binding-in-the-Marsh,
We've got a rather serious confession,
At Much-Binding-in-the-Marsh,
By subterfuge we'll see next June's procession,
We've hired a horse's outfit for the Coronation
  Day,
We've bribed the Royal coachman not to give our
  game away,
We'll be shouting "Good old Charlie!"
From inside a Windsor Grey,
At Much-Binding-in-the-Marsh,
(I'm the front legs!)
Much-Binding-in-the-Marsh,
(I'm the back legs!)
MUCH (two, three, four!)
BIND - ING - IN - THE
MARSH!'

9 mistaken identity

No one would ever have said that, at any time in Kenneth's life, success 'turned his head', and yet Joan found that a strange metamorphosis seemed to come over him after the initial success of 'Much-Binding'.

In 1944, he met a new lady, and, quite inexplicably, fell madly in love again. Her name was Mrs Marjorie Thomas. She was even smaller in stature than Joan, a brunette, the young widow of a certain Lieutenant George Thomas of The Rifle Brigade, who had been killed at Calais. There was one child of the marriage, a daughter, Susan, born in 1939, who never knew her father.

George Thomas appears to have been a gentleman of some substance, and, if there was any consolation to be derived from this tragically brief marriage, it was that his widow was left very comfortably provided for. Not that I am suggesting for one moment that this influenced Kenneth's attraction for Marjorie.

Marjorie lived during the war, and for some years afterwards, in what might appropriately be described as a 'luxury flat' in Cottesmore Court, W.8, where she also had the benison of an incomparable nanny, who

not only cared for and supervised every moment of
Susan's life, but also ran the household.

The story of Kenneth's first meeting with Marjorie
sounds too improbable to be true.

Some time in 1944, Mrs Thomas had attended a
cocktail party where she had met and talked to (as far
as one can ever talk to anybody at a cocktail party) a
most amiable man, whose name she recollected later,
was Kenneth Horne. She remembered he was a wing-
commander, and he had told her that he worked at the
Air Ministry.

Some weeks later, giving a party of her own, she
found herself in that well-known predicament shared
by every hostess in her time, in search of a spare man.
She cast her mind back. Who was that nice chap she
had met at that awful bun fight? What was his name?
Kenneth Horne, of course! She dialled the Air
Ministry number.

'Wing-Commander Horne.'

'Oh, hallo, is that Kenneth Horne?'

'It *is*.'

'Oh, I hope you will remember me. I'm Marjorie
Thomas, and we met at a party a week or two ago. I
wondered if you might be free next Tuesday. I'm
giving a little party, and I'd love you to come.'

I don't have to spell it out for you, do I? He knew
perfectly well that never in his life had he met anyone named Marjorie Thomas. But she sounded rather
nice. It was the kind of situation he simply couldn't
resist.

'How jolly nice of you,' he said. 'That sounds delightful. *What's* the address, again?'

'10, Cottesmore Court.'

'Of *course*! Thank you so much, I'll look forward to it.'

He duly presented himself at the party.

'What name shall I say, sir?' asked Nanny.

'Wing-Commander Horne.'

She led him towards Marjorie. 'Wing-Commander Horne, madam.'

Marjorie looked bewildered.

'But—' she gasped, 'you're not Kenneth Horne.'

'Oh yes I am.'

'Was it you I spoke to on the telephone?'

'Come to think of it,' he said, 'it *must* have been. I'm sure I recognize your charming voice.'

She gave up. 'Well, do come in and have a drink.'

He stayed until the guests were thinning out.

'Are you free later this evening? I'd love to take you out to dinner.'

He took her out to dinner. The first of innumerable times. It was not until some time later that he met his namesake. The dramatist (then Wing-Commander) Kenneth Horne, who, as it happened, also worked at the Air Ministry.

Joan spent two leaves with him in 1944, and during the second of these she knew unmistakably that he was in love with somebody else. It was a bitter shock to her, and she found it almost impossible to believe. She had become aware that her own environment of life in the W.A.A.F. had probably changed her, she had grown up, and found her independence. She had had a few mild little swings with two or three chaps during this time, but they were quite light-hearted and had left her unscathed. Kenneth was still 'her man', and she thought he felt the same about her.

So, when the full impact of this awful discovery hit her, she didn't know quite what to do, and it was only after long deliberation that she was finally driven to the inescapable conclusion that there would have to be a divorce. There was no rancour or vindictiveness in this decision. Had Kenneth made the smallest effort towards salvaging their marriage, she would probably have gone along with him, and been prepared to forgive and try again.

But the easier course for him was to let it ride; so, when she asked him point-blank: 'Do you want me to divorce you?', he could only answer: 'I suppose it would be best.'

Which was the reason why, some weeks later, at Claverton Manor, Edmund King's telephone rang, and the slightly breathless voice of a W.A.A.F telephonist announced:

'I have Wing-Commander Horne on the line for you, sir.'

'Put him through,' said Edmund.

They exchanged greetings, and then:

'Edmund, I wonder whether you might be able to help me. I saw Joan a week or so ago, and she has agreed to divorce me. Now, I'm told the simplest way to go about it is for me to give her evidence; you know, the old hotel bedroom routine. D'you think you could fix me up? I thought it might be better to do the whole thing down there, do you see, and I wondered if you might know a suitable hotel, and of course I suppose I shall have to find some *girl*.'

'Well,' said Edmund. 'I'll see what I can do. I daresay I could fix something. Leave it with me; I'll ring you.' He hung up.

Five minutes later, there was a knock on his office door. A rather pink-faced W.A.A.F corporal came smartly to attention in front of his desk.

'Yes, Corporal?'

'Squadron-Leader, sir—er—may I speak to you?'

'Yes. What is it?'

'I was on switchboard duty just now, sir, when Wing-Commander Horne rang. I somehow had my key down, sir, and—I'm afraid I heard your conversation, sir.'

'Did you, now!' said Edmund.

She went a slightly deeper shade of pink.

'I'm sorry, sir, but—well, about Wing-Commander Horne, sir, the *divorce* and all that. Do you think I could volunteer, sir?'

Edmund, almost exploding with suppressed laughter, busied himself over the papers on his desk.

'Well—er—thank you, Corporal. I shall have to speak to Wing-Commander Horne, of course. I'll let you know.'

She got the job. Edmund masterminded the whole operation, which went without a hitch. On the morning after the event, Kenneth telephoned.

'Edmund! Just to say thank you so much for everything. What a jolly nice little girl! We played gin-rummy all night, and, d'you know, she beat me hollow!'

The divorce case came up in the spring of 1945. Joan was demobilized, and living at home with her parents. Her father brought her to London, and after it was over

MISTAKEN
IDENTITY

he took her for a holiday to the Imperial Hotel at Torquay, to cheer her up. It has to be called 'Fate' (what
else?) that, during that week, she met and fell in love
with a young R.A.F. bomber-pilot, who was convalescing in Torquay. They married later that year.

It gives me tremendous pleasure to report that they
are still living 'happily ever after'.

Kenneth courted Marjorie for the best part of two years.
She was an expensive lady, and it seems to have been a
fairly lavish courtship. He discovered a car-hire firm,
the proprietor of which, a Mr Percy Millea, could
supply and chauffeur a Rolls-Royce, and during 1944
and 1945, Percy was hired at least twice a week to take
them out in the evenings to dinner and the theatre.

He had very soon met Miss Susan Thomas, then five
years old, and it was love at first sight. He, the only
father she had ever known; she, the child he had always
longed for. Susan has told me that, sadly, never in her
life was she close to her mother; she adored Kenneth
to the day he died.

The decree absolute came through. They named the
day. Friday, November 2nd, 1945. The place, Caxton
Hall, Westminster. It was the quietest wedding imaginable.

Dickie was to be best-man. The Rolls-Royce, with
Percy Millea in attendance, collected Kenneth and
Marjorie. They then drove to the Bristol Grill, where
they were to meet Dickie. He failed to show up, and
finally they had to go without him. They arrived at
Caxton Hall and were married in the presence of Percy
Millea and the Registrar's clerk.

Kenneth moved into Cottesmore Court. He was now demobilized from the Air Force, and had returned to Triplex, in the position of Sales Director at the company's head office at 1, Albemarle Street.

This historic building, facing on to Piccadilly, was many years ago The Albemarle Hotel, a small discreet establishment where once there lived Mrs Lillie Langtry ('The Jersey Lily'), and where His Majesty King Edward VII was a frequent visitor. I leave to your imagination the fine crop of ribaldries which has blossomed during the Triplex Company's tenancy of the building, since its conversion into offices more than sixty years ago.

If anyone ever imagined that Kenneth's post-war appointment at Triplex was in the nature of a sinecure, and secondary in importance to his career as a prominent radio celebrity, they could hardly be more mistaken. All his ex-colleagues and fellow directors in this company, without exception, have confirmed the fact that his business career always took precedence. He was a first-rate business man, immensely hard working, who gave unstintingly of his time and his expertise to the company. He was in his office at nine o'clock every morning, and he seldom left before five-thirty.

Mr Ralph Hewson, the present Sales Director of The Triplex Safety Glass Company, was recruited into it in September 1946 by Kenneth himself, as a progress controller at the Willesden factory. He had a dedicated respect and devotion to Kenneth, which was total. To quote him: 'I would have gone to the ends of the earth for him.'

MISTAKEN
IDENTITY

One of his earliest memories is of the winter of 1947, one of the severest of this century. The factory at Willesden was frozen up, and unbearably cold. The work-force there were working in overcoats, with whatever auxiliary heating they could scrounge. In the middle of the worst week, Kenneth made a point of going to Willesden from the warmth and comfort of his office in Albemarle Street, to share their misery and try to cheer them up. Neither was it a fleeting token visit. He stayed there working on progress reports for the whole day.

Ralph Hewson had been there for barely a year, and still felt himself very much of a new boy, when Kenneth sent for him to discuss a replacement for the Sales Manager, who was moving to another company.

'I wondered whether you might have anyone in mind for the job, Hewson?'

'Well sir, I don't really think I have. Perhaps you ought to look outside; unless you might think of promoting the office manager?'

'No. I don't want him in that job. I've given a lot of thought to this, and I've made up my mind. How would you like to have a bash at it?'

Ralph Hewson had, as he puts it, 'hardly got his feet under the table'. It was a great opportunity. He worked ten times harder than he needed to. Kenneth gave him an enormous lot of advice and help. He was always open to listen to every problem. Though once he said, with that well-known twinkle

'Don't take it *too* seriously, Hewson. Work must be *fun*. You can't win 'em all, you know!'

He remembers the many business journeys he made

with Kenneth, to attend sales conferences, and meet important customers. Petrol was difficult in those days, and for the longer journeys they travelled by train. One of the things which struck him was the number of porters Kenneth seemed to know by name on practically every station. He was a keen sender of telegrams.

Once, at a stop on a journey, he put his head out of the carriage window, looked around, and then called:

'Fred! Hey, Fred!'

A porter came at the double to the carriage.

'Hallo, Mr Horne.'

'Fred, be a good chap and send off this telegram for me.' (pressing a pound note into Fred's hand!)

'Certainly sir. Right away!'

Triplex always had a stand each year at the Farnborough Air Show, which Ralph Hewson was responsible for organizing and supervising. Kenneth would visit this, and spend a lot of time there. He was always encouraging and appreciative of everything which Hewson had done, but in addition there would be a telegram which arrived on the stand an hour or so after his departure:

'First class show Hewson. Carry on the good
work best of luck. K. H.'

There was a certain ugly incident which occurred within the company, when a member of the sales staff appeared to go completely round the bend, got blind drunk, took away a car belonging to a representative of one of the company's important customers, vanished for several days, and, when finally caught up with, was found to have sold it. If anyone had really put his mind to working out a fool-proof method of getting fired and blacked for life, this surely had to be it.

In due course the miscreant was summoned to the Sales Director's office, where he spent a long time. Later, Ralph Hewson was called in to hear the result of this interview, which he was very distressed about since the man was a member of his department.

Kenneth said: 'Well, I've had a long talk to him. I'm afraid we *can't* keep him in sales, but he's not a bad chap really, and he's had a good record up to now, so I don't want to sack him. I've got him a good job in the factory, and he's promised to work hard and gradually pay back the money this little lark has cost us.' He paused for a moment. Then he said quietly:

'You know, Ralph, "there but for the grace of God ..."!'

There was only one occasion when he ever came near to confessing himself to Ralph Hewson. They were waiting for a train on Southampton station, having a cup of tea in the refreshment-room. He was quiet and preoccupied, and suddenly he said:

'You know, Hewson, within reason I can have pretty well anything I want; and yet, I'm not happy. Life's jolly difficult, isn't it!'

Poor Hewson, whose relationship hitherto had never exceeded the bounds of subordinate to senior executive, was slightly nonplussed to find himself suddenly thrust into the position of confidant, and said tentatively:

'I'm—er—sorry to hear that, sir. Can I—help in any way?'

Kenneth, realizing that he had unwittingly embarrassed him, chuckled ruefully.

'My dear chap, I don't know what came over me. Yes, of course you can help. Buy me another cup of tea. Or tell me a filthy story!'

In fact, he hardly ever told a dirty joke, though if they were funny he had a keen appreciation of them. With all his sophistication he had a certain element of schoolboy humour, which is illustrated by a gag he tried on Ralph Hewson. He drew on his scratch-pad a triangle, with sides about two inches long, and the base one inch. He then said: 'I want you to write along the left side of the triangle the words: "What did John".' Hewson wrote. 'Now, along the right side you write: "Say to Mary".' Hewson wrote again. 'Now', said Ken, 'along the base you must write: "On the first night of their honeymoon".' Hewson took the pencil, paused, and remarked: 'There's not much room to get it in, is there!' Ken roared with laughter, took out his diary and wrote down Hewson's last remark. 'I'm making a collection of the comments,' he said. 'I've got some beauties!'

His two careers were strictly segregated. There was a tacit understanding that nobody talked about the radio shows in the office. The most that ever happened would be for Hewson to say:

'Enjoyed it last night, sir.' To which Ken would reply:

'Good show! We thought it was great fun. Now, what have we got today?'

The 'Much-Binding' scripts were more often than not written with Dickie at The Royal Automobile Club during the lunch hour. They would sit in the writing-room, one on either side of a double desk, and great guffaws of laughter have been known to shatter that sacred calm. They then met again on Sunday to put the script together for the broadcast on the following Tuesday.

Everybody in the entertainment world knew that Ken was, vaguely, 'a director of Triplex', and nobody really cared. Conversely, business customers with whom he came in contact seemed to care far more that their eleven o'clock appointment was the same chap who had made them roar with laughter on the wireless just the evening before, and probably to a certain extent were apt to dine out on it. I am not saying he wouldn't have achieved the same results in business anyway, but there is no doubt at all that his success and popularity as a broadcaster enormously enhanced his position in business. So many people have said: 'Kenneth could call on any of the biggest motor manufacturers and be shown straight into the Chairman's office.'

It was the same story everywhere. He was their friend, and he always made them laugh.

These were the years when he was steadily establishing himself more and more successfully in every sphere of his life, and understandably his life-style reflected this success. He had a young attractive wife, and a glossy background (characterless and impersonal, but appropriate!). He was always immaculately dressed in public, with the inevitable clove carnation in his button-hole, though in private he revelled in the oldest and scruffiest garments, in which he was happiest.

There was a certain pair of grey flannel trousers, to which he was particularly devoted, which Marjorie

highly disapproved of. Twice she consigned them to
the dustbin, each time Kenneth salvaged them protest-
ing. Finally Marjorie cut them into several pieces
before throwing them away. Kenneth found the pieces
while Marjorie and Susan were out. When they returned, they saw on the hall table a mound of small
pieces of grey flannel, and, propped up in the middle, a
small cross made of matchsticks.

'What on earth is this?' asked Marjorie.

'That,' replied Kenneth, 'is a memorial to my poor
old flannels. What a rotten thing to do!'

By 1947 he had achieved his first Rolls-Royce. One
of the smaller models, and he drove it himself, but no
Rolls-Royce is mere!

His home life was minimal. He and Marjorie dined
out three or four times a week, though, if this sounds
like riotous living, it should be remembered that his
entertainment career probably took him out three or
four times a week.

He was up at eight each morning, and always got his
own breakfast. Marjorie's domestic chores were not
unduly taxing.

He was enchanted with his new-found daughter and
showered her with treats, though he remained dis-
creetly aloof from any serious part of her upbringing.
Susan has many endearing memories of him. At the
age of nine she was invited to model some children's
clothes for a Bond Street shop, and, for the first time
in her life, paid the princely fee of five pounds. With
this enormous sum burning a hole in her pocket, her
sole idea was to buy a very special present for her
mother and father. She had found out that what they

wanted were two rather special and very fine sherry glasses, and she asked to be taken by her mother to the shop where these could be found. Kenneth knew that the glasses had to be right, and that they would need unfailingly to be used by Marjorie and him. He also knew that they were bound to cost considerably more than five pounds. So he telephoned the shop, explained the situation, and asked that, regardless of the actual cost, whatever Susan chose should be priced to her at no more than five pounds, and that he would call at the shop on the following day and pay any balance outstanding.

Susan and her mother arrived at the shop, where they inspected a large number and variety of glasses. Finally they came upon the perfect pair. Marjorie extolled them, and confirmed that they were exactly what Daddy would like. Susan, in a somewhat tremulous whisper, enquired the price. The perfectly briefed shop-keeper, not batting an eyelid, replied:

'Those, madam, are just five pounds for the pair.'

They were carried home in triumph. Daddy was ecstatic! It was many years before she knew.

Two years later, having reached the advanced age of eleven, and having (perhaps as a result of Daddy's lavish indulgences), become slightly insufferable, she was packed off to boarding-school to probably one of the most exclusive establishments for young ladies, St James's, in West Malvern.

About half way through her second term, firmly established as a natural agitator, she persuaded her classmates to stage a sit-in strike, for a reason which today she cannot even remember. The particular system at this school required each class to move at the end of each period to another classroom, and when Susan and her strikers stolidly refused to budge, a major disruption set in.

The headmistress sorted it out somehow; but rightly deciding she would not suffer this sort of nonsense, she got straight away on the telephone to Susan's parents and delivered an ultimatum, suggesting that they had better come immediately to the school, either to persuade their rebel daughter to mend her ways, or to remove her forthwith.

Kenneth, as I have said, had never involved himself in any major policy decisions concerning Susan; but now Marjorie, ducking this fearful crisis and pronouncing it 'man's work', packed him off to Malvern.

Kenneth first saw the headmistress, and was fully briefed on the gravity of the situation.

'Disgraceful!' he agreed: 'Leave her to me. May I have her out this afternoon?'

He met her, with a beaming smile. He took her for a drive in the Rolls, before feeding her a huge tea. They chatted away happily. Not one word of reproof was spoken. Around six o'clock he delivered her back to the school. As he was saying goodbye, with an enormous hug, he whispered in her ear:

'Now, *try* and behave a bit better, will you?'

From then on she was exemplary.

10 "this thing called love"

In September 1948, Kenneth's secretary at Triplex was leaving to get married, and he required a replacement.

The successful applicant, after considerable competition and elimination, was a tall elegant young woman, whose cool efficient facade concealed a warm sympathetic humorous character. Her name was Joyce Davis.

Her first impression of her new boss:

'He was such a nice guy, you wanted to do everything you possibly could to help him. He was never cross or unreasonable and he had such a real appreciation of anything you tried to do.'

His personal filing system was chaotic! On her first day he asked to see a quite important letter from Pilkington Brothers which he needed to refer to. Poor Joyce searched the files, practically tore the office apart, and was almost crying with frustration when he put his head round the door.

'How are you getting on?'

'I *can't* find it!'

'You know, when in doubt, I always look under MISC.'

"THIS THING
CALLED LOVE"

Under MISC it was!

'Can I please have some more files?'

'Of course. As many as you like.'

Within a week, everything was running like clockwork, and MISC had almost faded away!

She adored working for him, and there is no doubt that they had an enormous amount in common. One of the first things she remarked about him was his total lack of pomposity and self-importance, and his facility for putting strangers completely at ease. Yet he was always aware of the occasions which merited some respect for his position and authority.

As Sales Director, he was often called upon to interview applicants for jobs in his department. Joyce developed an infallible intuition about each applicant's chances, by observing his approach to Kenneth. How *not* to succeed in business without even trying was to sweep confidently into the office, start off by calling him 'Ken', and then proceed to tell him a funny story. He once said to Joyce:

'You know, one more crack out of that joker, and I'd have told him, "Please don't stand on ceremony; feel free to call me Mr Horne!"'

He could always spot the man who really needed the job. He had his own code of important pointers.

It didn't matter if the shirt cuffs were a bit frayed, but it mattered vitally that the finger-nails were clean, and the shoes polished, and there was a certain sense of humility and good manners.

Kenneth soon discovered that Joyce was an enthusiastic tennis player. So, too, was his cousin Harry Pilkington, whose dynamic energy almost outstripped

"THIS THING
CALLED LOVE"

Kenneth's. In the summer of 1949, there used to be early morning tennis matches at 7.30 a.m., Harry and his daughter against Kenneth and Joyce. They would all return to the flat at the top of Selwyn House (the London headquarters of Pilkington Brothers), a beautiful Regency house overlooking St James's Park, where they changed and breakfasted before going to work. Joyce reverentially remembers Harry Pilkington as the only man she ever met who could carry on two conversations simultaneously while doing *The Times* crossword puzzle!

Joyce lived with her widowed mother and younger sister in a pleasant house in Barnet; where, to return hospitality, she once invited Kenneth and Marjorie for dinner. It was a good dinner, which Kenneth was clearly enjoying, when he noticed with some embarrassment that Marjorie was pushing the food around her plate, and eating nothing.

'Come along, darling,' he said. 'Eat up, it's jolly delicious!'

'I'm afraid I'm not very hungry,' said Marjorie, wanly. 'I'm so tired. I've been standing all day, having fittings for clothes.' (Turning to her hostess) 'It's exhausting, don't you think?'

Before Mrs Davis could think up the answer to this one, Kenneth had jumped in:

'I *know*,' he said. 'I had a fitting for socks today, absolutely ex*haus*ting!'

Yet he had an immense loyalty to Marjorie. He never opposed her, nor asserted his authority against her. He indulged her in everything, showering her with expensive presents, expensive holidays, every outward

84

trapping, to reassure himself that the marriage was a success, as year by year went by, and he knew in his heart that it wasn't, and he was falling more and more in love with Joyce.

Cryptically, he once asked her:

'Why didn't you clock-in earlier?'

A close friend (in this context he must remain anonymous), who had known him intimately during his marriage to Joan, once said to him:

'You know, Ken, I never understood why you married Marjorie.'

Kenneth grinned, paused for a moment, and then:

'Well old boy, I suppose I needed a change. You see, Joan only ever used to laugh at *most* of my jokes. Marjorie never laughs at any of 'em!'

He tried so hard to keep the illusion going. Christmas was always the high-spot of the year. Christmas Day was also Marjorie's birthday. And Christmas Eve was Kenneth's shopping day.

At 8.30 in the morning, the car would collect him, and he set off for a whole day of shopping. He returned home at 5.30 p.m., and a mountain of parcels would be carried into his dressing-room, where he shut himself up for several hours, wrapping up presents. Apart from the main presents for Marjorie and Susan, there were always extras, such as the very newest lighter, ball-point pen, kitchen gadgets, and inside every present was a special little message.

The only time he ever departed from this last minute shopping routine was one year when he decided he would give Marjorie a sheepskin jacket. Since she was so very small, he knew this must be specially made to order, so he enlisted Susan's help, and, some weeks ahead they took a coat from her wardrobe, for the measurements, and went off together to the shop. The skins were carefully chosen, the colour, the style, every small detail was meticulously discussed. They left the shop bubbling with excitement, it was a wonderful secret which they shared ... Christmas Day arrived, and the brightly wrapped box was presented to Marjorie. She tore off the wrappings and looked in the box.

'Oh, thank you,' she said with a marked lack of enthusiasm, 'very nice.' She didn't even take the coat from the box.

Poor Kenneth's face collapsed like a punctured balloon.

11 declaration of independence

B y the end of the 1940s the motor industry was booming, and so, as a vital part of it, was Triplex. Kenneth was immensely successful and carried great responsibility in the company.

In 1950, he acquired his next Rolls Royce, and, as befitted his position, he decided he also needed a chauffeur. By chance one day, in Jermyn Street, he spotted Percy Millea. I somehow don't imagine that Percy needed very much persuasion to come and work for him permanently. The job lasted for the next eight years.

The Triplex Company, although in fact autonomous, was very closely concerned with Pilkington Brothers. Kenneth's cousin (at that time Sir Harry Pilkington) as well as being chairman of the family company, also served on the board of Triplex, and was a member of the sales committee. In this way he was in constant touch with Kenneth, and was impressed with his exceptional ability.

Sir Harry was President of the Federation of British Industry, and in those days there was an annual Fair, which was promoted as a shop-window for British goods, in two sections. One for heavy engineering exhibits, which was staged in Birmingham by the Birmingham Chamber of Commerce; the other, for light industries, was presented in London, under the aegis of the Government.

Industry as a whole had lost confidence in the way this Fair was run by the Board of Trade. It was an important source of obtaining overseas trade, but, in the best tradition of Whitehall, the civil servants could never arrive at speedy decisions so essential in industry, where time is often vital.

So, early in 1954, it was decided to hand over the promotion of the Fair to private enterprise, with financial support from the Government, and a new company called B.I.F. Ltd was formed.

It was agreed that there should be an advisory board of six honorary directors recruited from the top echelon of industry, and Sir Harry Pilkington, as President of the Federation of British Industry, was asked to make nominations. He chose as Chairman, Sir Ernest Goodale, a prominent figure in the textile industry; and the next four places on the board were filled by:

Sir Nutcombe Hume, of Charterhouse Investment Company, Mr W. J. Arris, of the Burroughs Office Machinery Company, Mr R. P. S. Bache, of George Salter & Co. Ltd. and Mr Reginald Whitehouse, then Chairman and Managing Director of The Chad Valley Company.

This left one place to fill, and without hesitation Sir Harry nominated his cousin, Kenneth Horne.

This caused something of a stir. Eyebrows were raised, questions asked. What had Mr Horne done in this particular field? Sir Harry, sticking to his guns, explained that Mr Horne was a man of tremendous drive, business experience, flair and personality, and, in the field of publicity, he would be of immense value. The Chairman of Triplex, Sir Graham Cunningham, was consulted, and agreed that Kenneth should be allowed to serve on this board for a term of one year.

The day to day working of the new company was conducted by a General Manager, a Mr J. Reading, seconded from the Board of Trade, who was responsible to his immediate superior Mr L. G. Balfour, who in turn was answerable to the President (which surely has to be the longest way round of arriving at a snap decision!). Mr Reading seemed totally out of his element in this new environment. A permanent civil servant, he had never, in all his working life, been required to take decisions. Although the overall reaction of industry in general was sympathetic to this new B.I.F. image, and anxious for it to prosper, they found it was still strangulated by the red tape of Whitehall.

With no progress being made, and the advisory board realizing that immediate action had to be taken, the directors sought, from the Government, permission to amend the articles of association to give themselves wider scope in running the company, and to appoint a full-time paid Managing Director, and to return the General Manager to the Board of Trade. This was agreed. A board meeting was called, and the Chairman and four directors unanimously nominated their colleague Mr Kenneth Horne to fill this new position.

DECLARATION OF
INDEPENDENCE

Sir Harry Pilkington's faith had not been misplaced. But this important executive job would obviously demand full time attention. Even Kenneth, leviathan for work as he was, could not possibly handle it in addition to his Sales Director's job at Triplex.

His position in the company seemed impregnable. He was 'The Dauphin', and, by every hereditary right, had to be in line for the top job of Chairman and Managing Director. On the most reliable authority I have been told that, had this natural progression taken place, Kenneth Horne would have become one of the most powerful figures in the motor industry. He would most certainly have been given a knighthood, and probably in due course a life peerage.

But he wasn't there yet. The Chairman and Managing Director was still, at that time, Sir Graham Cunningham, an able and experienced executive; but there is little doubt that he resented Kenneth's meteoric rise in those nine years since the war, and ... he was a martinet. He had a board of directors to the majority of whom his word was law.

Kenneth's proposition was that he should be seconded to the British Industries Fair for a period of two years.

Sir Graham Cunningham 'put it to the Board', and on the following day informed Kenneth that there could be no question of any short-term secondment, but that, if he wished to take up the B.I.F. appointment, the Board would accept his resignation from Triplex as of that day.

In all the years I knew him, I cannot remember ever seeing Kenneth angry. But there can be little doubt that, at that moment, he was. This was probably the biggest moment of destiny in his entire life. Had he made a different decision the whole course of his life would have been altered. He might, in fact, even have been alive today.

He was not irrevocably committed to the B.I.F. appointment, but they had undoubtedly made him a very attractive and lucrative offer. And, far more than this, he was, as ever, determined to remain his own master. So, after twenty-seven years, he left Triplex, and never went back.

12 change of direction

I F he never reached the pinnacle of power in the motor industry, he certainly achieved the pinnacle of popularity. In every branch of the industry, from the chairmen and managing directors of the big companies, the designers and engineers, the salesmen, the public relations officers, the technical press, wherever one turns even today his name is remembered with an affection which amounts almost to veneration.

He was never a name-dropper, though he had some heavy artillery to drop, had he had the inclination. Among the giants of industry who were his close friends were Lord Black, Lord Stokes, Sir George Harriman, Sir Alec Issigonis, Sir William Lyons, Lord Sieff, Sir Jan Lewando, Lord Mancroft, to name-drop but a few! He never dropped their names. It is more likely that they dropped his, and were proud of knowing him.

Alan Hess, the distinguished racing motorist of the 1930s, and for many years a prominent figure in motoring circles, has told me of a group of motor industry P.R.O.s who, in 1960, founded a small and very exclusive society called The Off-The-Record Circle, of which Kenneth was an honoured member. And this, bear in mind, more than four years after he had completely

CHANGE OF
DIRECTION

severed his official connection with the industry. The
Circle would meet every few months for dinner and
discussion in a private room, either at the R.A.C. or
L'Écu de France, where a remarkably good time was
undoubtedly had by all.

So he exchanged the Parish of St James for Ingersoll
House, Kingsway, where he immediately took up his
new job. Not quite as handy for nipping across to the
R.A.C. for a script-writing session with Dickie, but in
fact there were no more of these, because 'Much-Binding' had at last come to an end.

Just before we leave it, there are two stories about
Dickie which I am anxious to record for posterity. I
first met him more than forty years ago, and I have
always thought he had an air of slightly worried pre-
occupation. I therefore more than ever appreciated the
information that Kenneth had once christened him
'Colonel Vaguely'!

I also enjoyed the following snatch of conversation.

Murdoch: 'I had a very serious illness when I was
a kid.'

Horne: 'Did you live?'

Let me tell you the story about Edward Wilkinson,
who, as I mentioned earlier, 'made a name for himself'.
To be more strictly accurate, Kenneth and Dickie
made that name for him.

Edward had always made a point of listening to the
'Much-Binding' broadcasts, and, in the middle of one
programme, he had been astonished to hear Kenneth
say, apropos of nothing in the script:

'By the way, Murdoch, have you seen Edward Wilkinson lately?'

CHANGE OF
DIRECTION

It was obviously an impromptu line, because there was a fractional pause before Dickie picked it up, and replied:

'No, I haven't, sir. I think he's probably wintering in Sidi Barrani.'

From then on, 'Edward Wilkinson' seemed to crop up, totally unexplained, in practically every programme. Nobody had the faintest idea who 'Edward Wilkinson' was, or if, in fact, he actually existed. He was a sort of legendary 'Kilroy' character who was constantly 'here', though no one knew why. Listeners began to write in to the B.B.C. enquiring about him, and poor Edward got to the point of only having to announce his name for people to react with:

'Oh! Are you *the* Edward Wilkinson, from "Much-Binding"?'

At the height of his fame, he happened to be in London, and (as he always did) called to see Kenneth at his flat. During the visit, Kenneth said:

'I really must show you the Edward Wilkinson File. I have had letters from twenty different people named Edward Wilkinson, asking why I keep mentioning their name in "Much-Binding". I think you had better form an Edward Wilkinson Club, and hold an annual reunion dinner.'

At Christmas 1949, an astute young radio producer named Peter Cairns, then at the B.B.C. Midland Region at Birmingham, managed to nab Kenneth on one of his business trips there, as well as Edward (who lived in the city) and team them up together in a magazine programme called 'Around and About', where they sang a chorus of the 'Much-Binding' signature tune. It was Edward's one and only appearance at the microphone. Yet even now, more than twenty-five years later, he still gets asked the same old question.

Kenneth had several imaginary characters who frequently cropped up in his radio programmes. 'Edna Pirbright' and 'Gladys Wainwright' were just two of them. I wonder how many worried letters he had from *their* real-life counterparts?

Here is a short story, which I don't want to miss out, and, chronologically, it belongs near enough here.

In 1954, Kenneth heard that his friend and radio colleague Paul Jennings had been whipped into Midhurst Hospital with tuberculosis, and was recovering from an operation for the removal of a lung. He could have sent a get-well card, or a bunch of grapes. Paul would have been delighted. But he had a better idea. The following Sunday he collected a party of chums, Daphne Padell, Jerry Desmond, Joyce Davis, and drove them all to Midhurst in the Rolls. There he organized an impromptu entertainment for all the convalescent patients in the hospital. They played a panel game called 'Once Upon a Time', with Paul as chairman, and it went like a bomb.

Paul has never forgotten that Sunday. I don't suppose anybody else in that hospital, patients or staff, has either.

Kenneth threw himself whole-heartedly into his new job, and there is no doubt that his appointment attracted some favourable publicity, and gave the new company a shot-in-the-arm. But it was not enough. Such changes in the Articles of Association as were allowed were too few and too late. With all his personal drive and enthusiasm at full stretch, he found that industry was still disenchanted and unenthusiastic.

He had stipulated, as a condition of his new appointment, that Joyce Davis should be employed as his secretary, which had been readily agreed.

But Joyce had a mind of her own. With admirable strength of character, she saw this as the moment when she could force herself to break away and endeavour to make a new and different life. She was deeply in love with him, but she could see no possible resolution of this unhappy situation.

'If anyone had ever told me,' she said, 'that I was going to fall hopelessly in love with a bald headed man fifteen years older than I was, I'd have told them to go jump in the lake!' She had friends in Vancouver, and, within days of Kenneth's departure from Triplex, she flew out to them, and very soon found herself a job there.

She was absolutely right, of course, and, with hindsight, Kenneth himself would have been the first to see it. But at that moment he needed her desperately, and she left a terrible gap in his life; not only on an emotional plane, but because she had become indispensable to him in her professional capacity.

But nobody, in fact, is indispensable, and a highly capable replacement was found who was already working for B.I.F. as secretary to the General Manager.

Her name was Kathleen Haynes, known to her friends as Kate. She had every quality of the perfect

secretary, technical efficiency, tact and charm, and
devotion to her boss (though the latter was no problem!), and she filled her slightly invidious position
admirably.

He wrote constantly to Joyce in Canada, telling her
of all his problems. For a while she didn't reply, but
finally she relented, for she too was wretchedly unhappy.

During the brief reign of the B.I.F. as a private
company, the lavish hospitality of previous years to
visiting trade delegations and buyers was continued.
And who better to organize this than Kenneth, the
prince of hosts? The Royal Family, in the tradition
started by Queen Mary, continued to patronize the
Fair, through The Queen and The Duke of Edinburgh, The Queen Mother, The Duke and Duchess
of Gloucester, The Duchess of Kent, Princess Margaret
and Princess Alexandra. They bought a considerable
amount of merchandise during their visits, which
meant a lot to the exhibitors. It added to their prestige
to be able to tell overseas buyers that royal purchases
had been made at their stands. Kenneth, in company
with Sir Ernest Goodale, provided the escort for all
these royal visits.

There would also be evening receptions at Lancaster
House, and a banquet given by The Lord Mayor at
The Mansion House to Ambassadors and members of
the Diplomatic Corps, as well as trade delegations and
exhibitors.

Kenneth was achieving a lot through his contacts
and fresh approach; but, by early 1956, it became ap-
parent that more money from the Government was

going to be needed to keep the company going while trying to stimulate the flagging support. Despite the promises of Peter Thorneycroft (then President of the Board of Trade) to fight for the Fair, the Government suddenly decided to withdraw its backing.

Many of the staff of the B.I.F. had given up good jobs to help launch the company, believing that the Government support would give it a reasonable period in which to get established. They hardly got a fair crack of the whip. Many of them had the unenviable task of staging the final Fair, knowing they would be out of work when it ended.

None of these people could conceivably have reproached Kenneth personally, or held him in any way to blame. Yet he assumed full responsibility for them. He asked Kate to remain with him, saying that he would be the last man off the ship as he intended to see that everybody had a job to go to. He had never taken advantage of any friendship or influential contact in his life, but he spared himself nothing. He asked, badgered, and in some cases pleaded, until he achieved his goal, and nobody was unemployed.

Finally he set about finding a job for himself. There was no shortage of offers. But, emotionally, he was in a quandary, and he didn't know what he should do for the best.

From the short list which he considered, came an attractive invitation from Ford of Dagenham, proposing that he should become a roving ambassador and P.R.O., travelling the world for the company. He wrote to Joyce, asking for her opinion. Although it was the last thing she wanted, seemingly separating him irrevocably from her, she wrote back, strongly urging him to accept.

But there was one more offer to consider, about the least promising of them all, but it came from his colleague on the B.I.F. Board, Reg Whitehouse, Chairman of The Chad Valley Company, the toy manufacturers. He was in his late sixties, and ready for retirement. The company was going through a difficult period, and he begged Kenneth to join them as Chairman and Managing Director.

While he was considering this, he heard again from Joyce, saying she was returning to England, as her mother was ill. She was hoping to find a job in Public Relations. Perhaps this turned the trick. He talked to Reg Whitehouse, suggesting they should employ Joyce as P.R.O. to The Chad Valley Co., and Whitehouse agreed. He had previously asked Kate to remain as his secretary in whatever job he decided to go to. The following day he faced her in the office, and announced that it was to be Chad Valley.

She could not conceal from her face the utter amazement which she felt. He looked at her:

'You obviously think I've made the wrong choice.'

She hesitated. 'Well, since you ask me, yes, I do.'

'Tell me why.'

'Surely the other offers were so much better. But you really can't ask me. I have absolutely no right to try to influence you one way or the other in a decision as important as this. I'm only your secretary. If anybody has the prerogative to give you an opinion, surely it's your wife.'

He didn't reply.

13 brum again

BEFORE embarking on this new job he took himself
to France for a much needed holiday, leaving Kate to
hold the fort in the one remaining office of B.I.F. at
Ingersoll House during the final winding-up operations. It could only have been a coincidence that once
again he was to be working for a company which was
principally based in the city of Birmingham, for that
was where The Chad Valley Company had their fac-
tories and head offices. They also had some rather
dilapidated showrooms in the city of London, which
they were in process of evacuating pending the com-
pletion of new premises in Chandos Place. In the
interim, after Kenneth's return, he installed Kate in
a makeshift office at Cottesmore Court.

The Chandos Place showrooms opened with a
flourish in January 1957. It had been anticipated that
Kenneth would work from here for the first half of the
week, and in Birmingham for the latter part. But his
other career, in radio and television was still making
demands on his time, not that he ever allowed this to
overshadow his business life. He was always an in-
veterate traveller, seemingly unaffected by rail or road

journeys, and, to meet all his commitments, he was now often travelling to Birmingham and back three times a week.

One of the most important toy fairs, in which the company was naturally concerned, is held in Nürnberg in Germany, and it was obligatory that Kenneth should visit this for at least several days while it was in progress. But the journey to Germany assumed no more terrors for him than the journey to Birmingham, and, to fit in his broadcasting dates, he commuted just as happily day by day. He had worked for so many years at this tremendous pressure, that it had presumably become second nature to him.

The considerable cost of such peregrinations was of course charged to the company as a legitimate business expense, and was something which, certainly in the previous ten years, Kenneth had never even thought about. But, by comparison with the large scale companies which he had represented in those years, Chad Valley operated on a far more modest scale, and it seems that Kenneth's lavish expenditure of their limited resources caused them a certain amount of embarrassment.

The present Vice-Chairman of the Company, Mr Roger Swinburne-Johnson, served as a director with Kenneth, and speaks of him as 'a very enjoyable companion, who had a most stimulating effect on his colleagues and staff'. Whether, in fact, during his brief reign, he had as stimulating an effect upon the fortunes of the company, is more difficult to assess.

As though he hadn't got enough on his plate with this venture, he took on a totally new assignment when, in January 1957, he became the critic for the women's magazine *She*, writing a column of criticism from the male point of view, on each monthly issue.

Here is a selection from some of his columns, which bears his unmistakable stamp:

'"All Set For Spring" is the heading, and can you possibly imagine anything more repulsive than that coat? As far as the cloche hat is concerned, well ... I don't know, do you? I can think of some uses for it. Why don't people try and look like reasonable human beings instead of following these really ghastly fashions?'

'So they're going to have twelve TV programmes all about having babies, are they? Well, well, what on earth are we coming to? I suppose if it's going to make young married girls feel comfortable about having babies, then it is a good thing. But I don't think it's the sort of programme that I shall watch.'

'I don't know about you, but I'm getting a bit fed up with the Pill! The danger is that people will be told they are pregnant, and they will say: "Oh but I can't be—you see it said in *She* ..."'

'Looking back over what I have written, I feel that my reactions have been somewhat unenthusiastic, which is a pity because (and I mean this) there is a pleasant madness about this March *She*, coupled with a modi-

cum of sanity and a soupçon of education. By which
I mean that it's really a Gourmet and a Q.C. rolled
into one. And if that doesn't satisfy everyone, then my
name's not Nemesis T. Proudwater.'

It was a difficult year, and the stresses of it were mount-
ing more and more as it progressed. On February 25th,
1958, following a board-meeting in Birmingham, Roger
Swinburne-Johnson invited Kenneth to spend the night
at his house at Broad Campden in Gloucestershire.
Another director of the company, Eric Sutton, had a
daughter Pauline, a young actress who was appearing
in a play at Oxford. When Kenneth heard this, he suggested they should all drive over on that Tuesday night
to see her play, after which he would take them out for
supper. He had the Rolls, which he was driving himself. The arrangement was that he would take Roger
into Birmingham in the morning, before driving back
to London.

There was a heavy fall of snow in the night. At
breakfast the following morning when Kenneth appeared, Roger immediately noticed that he seemed far
from well.

'Good morning, Kenneth. Did you sleep all right?
You don't look too good.'

'Well, I didn't have too good a night, Roger. I woke
up with the most awful pins-and-needles in my left
leg. I can't seem to get rid of it. I do feel a bit poorly.'

'I'm so sorry. Would you rather not come into work?'

'Oh no. I'll be all right.'

They started off on the journey of some twenty-five

miles. Though driving the Rolls made no demands
upon his left leg, he was clearly in great distress.
Swinburne-Johnson offered to drive, but he would not
give in. By the time they reached the office he seemed
worse, and Swinburne-Johnson insisted that he should
go directly to a doctor in Birmingham, and that one of
the company chauffeurs should drive him.

An hour later, the chauffeur reported back to Swinburne-Johnson, that, on leaving the doctor, Mr Horne
had asked to be driven direct to the station, where he
had got on a train to London.

The identity of the Birmingham doctor seems to
have sunk into the mists of time, and only the vaguest
account of his diagnosis emerges, namely that Kenneth
had probably suffered a minor stroke. Several people
have criticized him for allowing Kenneth to make the
journey to London, saying that he should have sent
him immediately to hospital in Birmingham. I feel it
is more than likely that this is just what he did pre-
scribe. But he didn't know his casual patient at all; and
he didn't appreciate the insuperable difficulty of trying
to persuade Kenneth to do anything against his own
will. He had made up his mind to go home. So he
got himself on the train.

No first hand account of that journey has ever been
available, but it must have been a nightmare for him.
It is possible that he may have been alone in a first-
class compartment. It is hard to believe that anybody
seeing him in what must have been a state of such acute
distress could have failed to take some action to help
him. But he arrived at Euston, where he was found
in his compartment totally unable to move. He was

still conscious, and asked to be put into a taxi and driven to his own doctor, Dr John Gordon, in Wilton Crescent. Doctor Gordon realized immediately that he had a coronary thrombosis. With the minimum of delay he had him moved to a nursing-home in Queens Gate, where Marjorie was summoned. By then he was totally paralysed on his left side, and unable to speak. It was in this pitiful state that, on the following day, he celebrated his fifty-first birthday.

He was very seriously ill. He lay there like a log, a terrible grey colour, unable to speak, and his poor face had slipped.

Regrettably, Doctor Gordon died before this book was started; but Kenneth's physiotherapist, Mr Joe Friel, who was also a close friend, told me it was one of the worst strokes he had ever seen. He marvelled at the rapid and phenomenal recovery which Kenneth made, largely due to his own dogged determination to be well again. In less than two weeks he was out of the nursing home and convalescing at home. He was slowly regaining his speech. Joe worked by directly massaging the muscles of his face and neck, and also by mouthing words and making him mime their shape.

In later months he also had a course of treatment from a Canadian lady electro-therapist, which (I am reliably informed) was known as 'proprioceptive neuro-muscular facilitation technique'. The treatment received a lot of publicity, and the lady concerned was given rather more credit for Kenneth's recovery than she strictly merited. There is no question that it was Joe's initial perseverance and devotion which first set Kenneth on the road.

BRUM AGAIN

Practically his first breakthrough in restoring Ken's speech came at the end of a fairly heavy session, when he was giving him a general massage. Joe knew all his sensitive spots, and remembered, from earlier years, that the left thigh was the principal one. He suddenly grabbed this with considerable pressure. Kenneth emitted a strangulated yell, and then, clearly came the words: 'You bugger!'

Joe nearly cried for joy.

14 poco meno mosso

S o, painfully and painstakingly, he fought his way back, and after a while he was sufficiently recovered to be able to contemplate the future pattern of his life. Now Doctor Gordon faced him with a critical decision. He started off by telling him quite bluntly that he was lucky to be alive, but he had undoubtedly been taxing even his super-human capacity to an intolerable extent. He simply had to cut down. He offered him the alternative, a business career on a carefully modulated pattern, or some broadcasting. But on no account could he hope ever again to do both. It was a humiliating moment for Kenneth, for he realized that what John Gordon was telling him was that he would never again be one hundred per cent fit, and physical fitness was something about which he cared passionately. But he knew the score. He knew from experience that it was impractical to think that he could satisfactorily undertake the sort of top-level business management, in which he had been engaged on any sort of restricted scale. It was far too demanding. Radio, on the other hand, was more flexible. Television, at that juncture, was not even considered. By early May, he had written to

POCO MENO
MOSSO

Roger Swinburne-Johnson and tendered his resignation from the board of Chad Valley. It was probably all for the best.

His financial position was not exactly buoyant. He had always lived at an extravagant rate, and the overheads were still there. It isn't so simple abruptly to change one's way of life, and it was a matter of pride and of principle that he wasn't going to accept defeat lightly. But he was quietly philosophical, and knew that the situation called for some adjustments.

As the first economy, which stuck out a mile, the Rolls must go, and so must Percy Millea. It was only two years earlier, in the palmy days of the B.I.F., that he had bought the very first brand new Silver Cloud, a magnificent machine, with two tone green coachwork, registered in Kingston-upon-Hull in order to provide a KH number-plate. He had tried for KH1, but nothing nearer than 6 was available. So KH6 it was. He must somehow have salted away this number, because it proudly re-emerged, six years later, and he then kept it for the rest of his life. He sold the Rolls, gave Percy a generous golden handshake and found him an immediate job. It was no good mucking about with a slightly less expensive car. He went all the way, and bought a second-hand Morris 1000, which was perfectly adequate.

Having made the decision that entertainment was going to be his sole career, he next set about organizing it. It must be said in fairness to the B.B.C. that they rallied round admirably, though it was hardly from any motives of charity that they were anxious to employ Kenneth Horne.

POCO MENO
MOSSO

His first reappearance was in May, as Chairman of 'Twenty Questions' during one of Gilbert Harding's retirements from the programme.

I had not known at that time what a challenge he found this to be. He had asked Joyce to come to the programme, but at the last moment she was prevented from doing so by being laid low with a cold. She and her mother were then living in a flat in Hays Mews. He called there on his way to the broadcast. He was limping rather badly, and using a stick, but he climbed the stairs to the flat, and sat by Joyce's bed. It was the only time she had ever known him in an acute state of nerves.

'Listen, my dear,' she said to him, 'calm down. You have nothing to worry about. You're Kenneth Horne! Everybody's rooting for you. They are going to be so overjoyed to see you back again.'

'But—I've got to *walk* on to that stage. They'll all see I *can't* walk properly.'

'Then, *don't* walk on. You can just go straight to your chair, and introduce the show from there.'

'That's almost worse. I've always walked on.'

'Then you'll walk on tonight. You're going to be fine. Stop worrying. Now off you go. I'll be listening.'

I was at The Paris before he arrived. I so well remember seeing him come down that staircase. He was using a stick. I have used one for the past thirty years. Rather alarmingly, he practically galloped down the stairs, as if to prove there was nothing wrong. I greeted him warmly. He waved the stick in the air.

'Snap!' he said.

POCO MENO
MOSSO

'Very distinguished,' I replied. 'All the best people use them.'

He laughed. 'I shan't need mine much longer.'

It came up to starting time. The producer went on the stage.

'... and here to introduce you to the team, we are pleased to welcome back Kenneth Horne!'

He dropped his stick. He went on to the stage with a kind of prowling stride, as though he was deliberately being funny.

The audience rose to their feet and cheered.

During 1957 there had been an approach for him to do a new radio comedy show, as anchor-man, and a pilot-programme had been recorded. This seems to have been shelved, largely, one imagines, on account of Kenneth's tremendous pressure of work in his Chad Valley job. Now negotiations were reopened, and discussions took place with writers Eric Merriman and Barry Took and producer Jacques Brown. In June 1958 it was decided to make another pilot, and the cast which was assembled for it, in addition to Kenneth Horne, was Kenneth Williams, Hugh Paddick, Betty Marsden, Ron Moody, singer Pat Lancaster, and a close harmony rhythmic group The Fraser Hayes Four, who, to my mind were one of the most outstanding and accomplished groups ever to be heard in British radio. The whole show was accompanied by the B.B.C. Variety Orchestra, conducted by Paul Fenoulhet. Digressing for a moment, as I now set down on paper this scintillating list of names, I am moved to shed a silent tear for the departed glories of B.B.C. Radio. How long ago it is, alas, since anything approaching this standard of light entertainment was offered to the radio listener!

Ron Moody appeared only in the first few programmes of 'Beyond Our Ken', before being succeeded by Bill Pertwee who freely acknowledges that it was this show, and all that Kenneth did for him, which set him on the road to success as a radio performer.

Bill's rise had been comparatively meteoric. Only some ten years earlier he had been an enthusiastic amateur actor, a member of 'The Star Timers' Amateur Dramatic Society, in Barnet; and a fellow member of this society had been Miss Joyce Davis! Joyce claims no credit for Bill's success, though no one was happier to see him make it.

In 1954, he was writing some comedy material for one of the revues at The Watergate Theatre, in Buckingham Street, Strand. This was undoubtedly a great forcing-house for a lot of fine talent. It occurs to me as regrettable that this notorious name which was blazoned across the world some eighteen years later, couldn't at least have served to publicize this splendid little theatre at a time when it could have done with it!

Anyway! Bill wrote some material for The Watergate. Somebody dropped out of the show, and he was asked to come in. And having digressed this far, bear with me a moment longer while I tell you that (among my not inconsiderable collection of theatre programmes) I have discovered the programme of that very show, for which I find that I too had written a number.

This was Bill's very first professional appearance. Only three years later he was booked for a four-minute

POCO MENO
MOSSO

comedy spot in a radio show called 'Variety Playhouse',
starring Jack Hulbert and Cicely Courtneidge, compered by Kenneth Horne, and produced by Jacques
Brown, which launched him in 1959 into 'Beyond Our
Ken', and an association with Kenneth which he remembers gratefully to this day.

Kenneth was, to Bill's mind, the perfect broadcaster,
whom he honestly believes will never be replaced. 'He
was such a marvellous bloke to know; and so kind and
helpful to me when I first joined the show. The rest of
the cast were all established actors and broadcasters;
I was comparatively a new boy who had come from the
Variety and Summer Show scene. He was always per-
suading the writers to put in extra little bits for me
which would help to get me established in the show.
He reminded us all that our audience was in all quar-
ters of the world, not just in that dedicated little crowd
of supporters in the studio where the show was recorded. More than anything I shall remember his
greeting when one met him. It became a delightful and
happy event. He made you feel ten feet tall, and that
the world was a good place to be alive in.'

Kenneth Williams was approached to take part in
that pilot-recording, which was his very first meeting
with Kenneth Horne. He was puzzled by him, and not
immediately won over.

'Here was this strange establishment figure in a neat
dark suit, more like somebody from the Foreign Office
rather than a pro. They'd sent me a copy of the script,
which didn't seem very funny; rather old-fashioned, I
thought, and a bit concert party. We had a read-
through and it got a bit better; Kenneth seemed to

bring it to life. Anyway, the long and short of it was that they accepted the pilot, and a couple of weeks later we recorded the first programme of "Beyond Our Ken".'

And that first programme was the start of an association which continued over the next eleven years.

Kenneth Williams is a punctilious man, who, like all the best actors, treats his professional work very seriously. One of the golden rules is to arrive in plenty of time for rehearsals as well as performances. He was always one of the first to arrive at The Paris studio for broadcasts.

In the corridor, at the side of the auditorium at The Paris, is a small tea-bar for artists and staff, and it was Ken W's almost invariable routine to go to this and get himself a cup of coffee while waiting for the others to arrive. Almost invariably too, the next member of the cast to arrive would be Kenneth Horne, and one of Ken W's memories, which has remained clear in his mind, is hearing Kenneth, with his limp, clumping up the slight incline to the tea-bar, dropping his left hand on to his shoulder, and quietly greeting him with: 'Hallo, chum!'

Kenneth Williams had been broadcasting previously with Tony Hancock in 'Hancock's Half-Hour'. It was not a happy association. He had found Hancock touchy and difficult; always asserting his position as the star comedian who had to get the best laughs. Now working with Kenneth Horne gave him a totally new conception of comedy.

POCO MENO
MOSSO

'We just stood at the microphone and he handed me the laughs on a plate. I had no need to worry. It didn't matter if I got the laugh on the feed-line. He always topped it. "It doesn't matter who gets the laughs," he used to tell me, "as long as the show gets them." There is one word I would always use about Kenneth Horne, and that's "geniality". The geniality he created was astonishing.'

That 'strange establishment figure' never pushed, just quietly won the respect, admiration and devotion of the whole cast. Dramas would arise, fearful hysterical outbursts, people would sweep out of the studio in a temperament; Kenneth would slip quietly out after them. Five minutes later they would be back, the drama over, everybody happy.

Ken Williams also recalls Kenneth's incredible 'card-index' mind, in which there seemed to be stored every funny voice, every dialect, every comedy trick, which he knew that each member of the cast was capable of. At first read-throughs, when the script didn't seem to be very funny, producer Jacques Brown would come through on talk-back from the control room:

'It's *not* coming off the paper, dears! *Lift* it off the paper!' Kenneth would hiss at Ken W: 'Try that bit "Irish",'—or—'Do your "Noël Coward"!' Whatever it might be, he knew exactly what treatment a particular line needed to make it work, and he was never wrong. Furthermore, after he had got it right, he never failed to praise the person concerned, as though the whole interpretation had been his own idea.

'Beyond Our Ken' pioneered a completely new trend in radio comedy. Its talented cast established a collection of characters who gently lampooned radio types and personalities everybody recognized.

Do you, perhaps, remember those two jolly decent public school chaps, Rodney and Charles? ('Hallo Rodney!—Hallo Charles!') And 'Cecil Snaith', the commentator, describing in reverent tones some important public occasion, at which some disaster invariably occurred, from which he hurriedly extricated himself with: 'I now return you to the studio!'—a gentle send-up of the unflappable Richard Dimbleby. 'Ambrose and Felicity', the terribly genteel elderly couple; and 'Arthur Fallowfield', the horticultural expert, whose solution to every problem was: 'The answerr loys in the soy-il!' And, in the midst of them all, the Rock of Gibraltar, the never changing Kenneth Horne. He was occasionally called upon to play a character, and, regardless of whom it was intended to be, it turned out unmistakably as Kenneth Horne!

Eric Merriman and Barry Took wrote the scripts for the first two series. Towards the end of the second, they had some serious disagreement, for which each of them undoubtedly blamed the other. The result was they stopped working together. Poor Kenneth, in something of a quandary, wrote to Barry:

'I am so very sorry to hear that you and Eric have split. I see that we can't possibly continue to use both of you. At the same time we can't afford to *lose* both of you. I do feel it is only fair that Eric, as the senior writer, should be asked to continue. I do hope you will understand that, as far as I am concerned, there are no hard feelings, and I am sure we shall work together again.'

POCO MENO
MOSSO

Typically, Kenneth was very concerned about Barry, and anxious to find more work for him. He invited Barry to write a pilot script for Dickie Murdoch and himself, along the lines of the 'Much-Binding' formula. Barry tried, and admits he failed miserably. It wasn't his scene at all. So there was a gap in their association for three years. But they got together again.

Kenneth was very fond of Barry, and had a great respect for him as a writer. As for Barry, he idolized Kenneth, and his style of writing and comic invention became more and more tailor-made for him.

Barry has most generously given me access to some of the many letters and bits of 'Hornorobilia' which he received from Kenneth over a number of years; and I am delighted to be able to reproduce a selection of them here.

Today is the centenary of the Banbury Tart.
The occasion was celebrated at Banbury Cross by a display of local tarts organised by the Women's Institute.

A world record Ewcan, which is a Goanese fish, was today caught off the West coast of South America by some Madagascan fishermen who had strayed from their territorial waters. The Goanese Ewcan has that unusual name because, when caught, it is supposed to cry: 'Ewcan Go-an ... Ewcan go-an ...' The fish has been sent to a taxidermist.

The little lion on eggs disappears officially next week. Said a spokesman: 'The task of training lions to sit first on the ink-pad and then on the eggs has proved beyond us.'

(Letter with small-ad newspaper cutting attached)
'French stamps and letters 1849-1875, top prices paid'
Dear Mr Took,

I'm surprised that you should have inserted such an advertisement in The Times, *of all papers. I am told that the stamps have little or no value, but the other french articles fetch a big price, provided they are about 1853 and unperforated.*

Yours sincerely,
An Ex-Admirer.

Sir Knebworth Hunt, the famous climber who recently conquered the highest mountain in Katmandu, is now attempting a similar feat in neighbouring Dogmandont. And from a message just handed in, I see he has reached the Peke.

Mavis M'Booloo, the Bessarabian pianist, arrived at London Airport today at noon precisely. She came at the invitation of B.O.A.C. to play the Minute Waltz in the canteen, and returned to Bessarabia at one minute past twelve.

Two cows have opened a boutique in Smithfield Market. It's called 'Boeuf a la Mode'.

POCO MENO
MOSSO

This evening in Teddington High Street, an alsatian dog which was supposed to be seeing its master home from the local was observed to be walking very unsteadily and hiccoughing. When stopped by a policeman, the dog refused to take a breathalyser test and said that its unsteadiness was due to mixing Kennomeat, Kitticat, Paws and Pedigree Chum, all enriched with too much Marylebone High Street.

A packed house greeted Miss Cynthia Pubes at Twickenham Scouts Hut tonight. The unusually large attendance is thought to have been due to misprints in the poster advertising Miss Pubes' lecture. The subject, instead of being 'Your Duties to Reading, was erroneously given as 'Two Cuties from Reading'.

One of Kenneth's lesser known accomplishments was after-dinner speaking, for which he had a tremendous flair and was in great demand.

Lord Mancroft, himself a past master in this field, found it worth taking some tips from Kenneth on the technique of public-speaking.

For example, Kenneth would never refer in a speech to a news-item which had only just appeared in that evening's newspaper. 'You can be *too* topical,' he said. 'Never use today's paper; always yesterday's, to give more of your audience a chance of knowing what you are talking about.'

Lord Mancroft considered Kenneth one of the best after-dinner speakers he had ever heard. He always took an immense amount of trouble with his facts, and find-

27. Sir Harry Pilkington (later Lord Pilkington of St. Helen's).

3. (*Opposite*) Joyce Davis.
9. (*Below*) With Kenneth at Triplex.
. (*Bottom*) The Off-The-Record Circle. (An off-the-record picture!)

9. (*Opposite below*) A Dog's Life!
ize-giving at a dog show.
eft) Brian Johnston, and (*right*) Stanley Dangerfield.

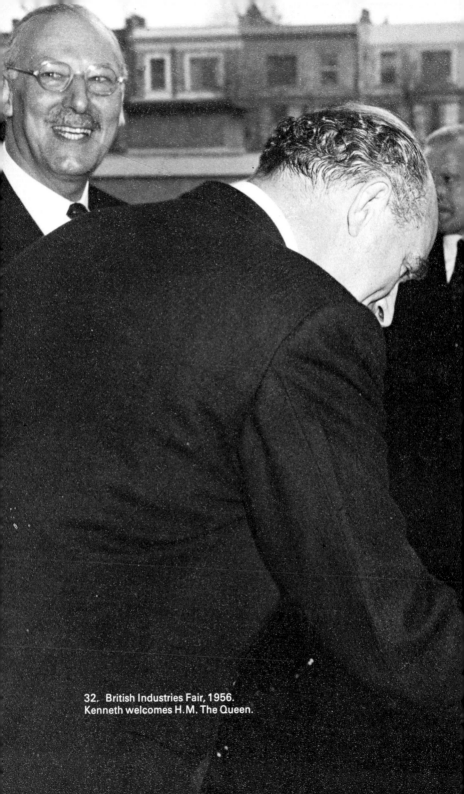

32. British Industries Fair, 1956.
Kenneth welcomes H.M. The Queen.

33. At Chad Valley, with Gilbert Harding.

(*Opposite*) "Two Many Cooks".
34. (*Top*) Advice from Philip Harben.
35. (*Below*) Trying it out.

36. & 37. (*Above and below*) "Twenty Questions", 1962.

"Beyond Our Ken". 1958-!
38. (*Above*) "It's rather a bad line
Hugh Paddick, Ron Moody, Kenneth Williams, K
39. (*Opposite*) "Cheese
(*From top*) Bill Pertwee, Pat Lancaster, Hugh Paddi
Kenneth Williams, Betty Marsden, K.

40. "Round The Horne." 1968.
(*Left to right*) Hugh Paddick, Kenneth Williams, K.H., Betty Marsden, Douglas Smith.

41. & 42. "Sturtles", Alciston, Sussex.
43. & 44. (*Opposite top*) "What sort of a mug do you take me for?"
(*Below*) "And this is my nesting-box!"

45. See you around !

ing out in advance about the people in his audience.

Kenneth said: 'Public speaking is rather like a duck swimming along very smoothly on the surface of a pond, and paddling away like mad underneath!'

Kenneth was also an expert interviewer; and, in a letter to a friend, Jane Page, an enthusiastic amateur anxious to break into radio, he gave his cardinal rules on the technique of interviewing, as follows:

'Don't forget that the good interviewer:

a. Prepares questions in advance.

b. *Listens* while the interviewee is talking.

c. Is ready to amend (a.) as a result of (b.).

d. Talks as little as possible. It is his job to give the proper questions, lead the interviewee on, and make him feel at ease.

e. *Never* interrupts. Even an "I see" or a "Yes" is annoying.

f. Makes quite sure the interviewee has completely finished one particular subject before he starts on the next.'

15 reprise

I HAVE mentioned that after the stroke in 1958 he had sold the Rolls and salted away that talisman number-plate KH6. It took him just five years to climb back to the top, and by 1963 he had acquired a gleaming black Bentley, which became the second KH6. He bought it on the strength of having had, in that year, the most prosperous time of his whole career, which is a remarkable standard of achievement from nothing but radio and television work. He bought the Bentley, I think, for his own personal satisfaction, and I hope it gave him pleasure. He didn't keep it all that long because he found it too much of a liability without a chauffeur to look after it. By 1967, having made his point, he exchanged it for a 4-litre Daimler, which became KH6 the third, and his very last car. But, let's face it, three Rolls-Royces, a Bentley and a Daimler is not a bad score for a man who started out with a motorbike and sidecar.

'Beyond Our Ken' came to a rather turbulent end in February 1964, by which I do not imply that it had been anything but a resounding success. The turbulence was strictly private and backstage, but the result of it was to create a long delay. Finally it was decided to rehash the original format, and Barry Took was invited to write the scripts with Marty Feldman. The cast remained basically unchanged. Ron Moody had earlier left 'Beyond Our Ken', and been succeeded by Bill Pertwee, who continued in the new show. Douglas Smith who, in 'Beyond Our Ken' had remained a fairly orthodox announcer, now came into his own in a variety of improbable parts and effects. The main change, to my mind a great improvement, was the title. It was now called 'Round The Horne' which Barry had dreamt up and nursed since long before 'Beyond Our Ken'.

Barry admits that he and Marty approached this new assignment with some trepidation. 'Beyond Our Ken' had established a big reputation, and they were well aware that everybody would be gunning for them and only too ready to make comparisons. But they needn't have worried. The show took on a new lease of life, and together they wrote no less than fifty scripts, before Marty Feldman dropped out to write and perform in his own brilliant television series 'Marty'. Barry continued, with some assistance from Donald Webster, Johnnie Mortimer and Brian Cooke, for a further sixteen shows.

The greatest innovation in this new show was the introduction of those two spectacular characters 'Sandy and Julian', which marked a breakthrough in the permissiveness of the B.B.C. When they first appeared in the script, John Simmonds, who had now taken over as producer from Jacques Brown, looked up at the read-through and announced in somewhat hushed tones:

REPRISE

'We shall have to go very carefully with these characters, or we're liable to offend people.'

Marty sprang to his feet. 'Bloody rubbish!' he shouted, 'Play 'em dead straight, bring 'em out into the open. What are you afraid of?'

He was right, of course. 'Sandy and Julian' were outrageous as characters, but they were also hilariously funny and, to my mind, never even mildly offensive. The anticipated letters of complaint arrived; but they were insignificant in comparison to the thousands of appreciations. I think what contributed to the success of 'Sandy and Julian' was their juxtaposition to that solid establishment figure Kenneth Horne. The way he played to them was masterly; totally unaffected, mildly surprised, but always innately polite. The combination was magical.

Every member of the cast was generously served by authors Took and Feldman, but they certainly made the very most of the characters they were offered. Let me just refresh your memory, for, as I write, it is already seven years since we last heard them, and there may well be some who sadly never did.

'Julian' was Hugh Paddick, 'Sandy' Kenneth Williams. Betty Marsden, fresh from her triumphs as 'Fanny Haddock' in 'Beyond Our Ken', now emerged as 'Daphne Whitethigh', a hoarse voiced fashion plater and sometimes cookery expert. Then Betty was 'Dame Celia Molestrangler', who, with her fellow thespian 'Binkie Huckaback' (Hugh Paddick) appeared as 'Fiona and Charles' in those 'too too terriblah' exaggerated Noël Coward situations. Finally (apart from a casual variety of a dozen or so one line characters), Betty

also appeared fairly regularly as 'Lady Beatrice
Counterblast (née Clissold)' a much married, much
divorced ('many *many* times!') ex-Gaiety girl, living in
seclusion at Chattering Parva, served occasionally by
her octogenarian butler 'Spasm' (Kenneth Williams)
who also played: 'Chou-en-Ginsberg. M.A. (failed).
Fiendish Japanese mastermind', 'J. Peasemould Gruntfuttock, the walking slum', and that perfectly horrific
folk-singer 'Rambling Syd Rumpo', not forgetting (unfortunately) 'Seamus Android, that bundle of wistful
Irish charm', so nauseatingly purveyed by Bill Pertwee
who also ...

What one tended to forget was that, in this gigantic
cast of thousands, there were in fact just four immensely
talented and versatile performers, plus the master
showman, who played all those other characterizations
of Kenneth Horne so brilliantly.

The show was built around him. Everybody knew
that. It couldn't have happened without him. Yet he
was never 'the star'. He had an enormous appreciation
of, and genuine gratitude to, all his fellow artists. His
generosity to them was prodigious. At the end of every
series of 'Round The Horne' he would always give the
most lavish luncheon parties, usually at the Hyde Park
Hotel, for everyone connected with the show, with
presents by every place. I reproduce one of his better
letters of invitation.

14th April 1967.

Dear Barry,

        Monday, June 12th is an occasion of
world shattering importance.

There will be Rabbi titillating at Cockfosters. Foster titillating at his own convenience. And cock-baiting at Mirabile Dictu.

Other items of interest on that day will be a screwing competition during the Carpenters Ball at Nailsworth; Taxidermist stuffing at Welwyn; Haddock Smoking at W. D. & H. O. Wills, and Favour currying at Veeraswamy's. There will be the usual jumble sale at Fortnum and Mason's, and a toupée demonstration at the Wigmore Hall —which will include a lecture by Sir Francis Horne entitled 'Round the Chichester'.

And by some quirk of fate there will be a 'Round the Horne' lunch in the Loggia Room at the Hyde Park Hotel at 1.15 p.m. (or nearest) on the same day.

Let me know if you can come—list of invitees overleaf, in case you want to avoid anyone.

All the best,
KENNETH.

From my own experience, I can say that the same thing happened after each series of 'Twenty Questions', and what superb parties they were! To say it was a pleasure to work with him is an understatement. It was also a privilege, and an unforgettable experience.

In 1965, Kenneth joined John Ellison as the second question-master in the long-running radio Schools Quiz, 'Top of the Form', which was a taxing job even for a fit man, involving as it did long journeys each week. At the end of that series, John thought up a new idea for a quiz, which he originally called 'Happy Families'.

It was a light-hearted affair in which families from the general public competed against show-business families on a knock-out tournament system. Kenneth was the chairman.

They first made a pilot for B.B.C radio, who seemed to like it, but, John tells me, were 'slow in making up their minds'. (Well, fancy!) So Kenneth took it to Southern Television, who jumped at it and did a short trial series. It was very successful, but John thought it would be even better to match the celebrity families against each other. So, for the next series, they changed the title to 'Celebrity Challenge', and a lot of very distinguished challengers took part, including, of course, Kenneth's old sparring partners Dickie Murdoch, with his son Tim (Kenneth's godson), and his daughter Belinda; Maurice Denham, his son and daughter; and Sam Costa, son and daughter, who reached the final of one series before being eliminated.

They also had, one week, Clement Freud with his wife and daughter, a phenomenally brainy child and something of a highbrow. Chatting to Kenneth before the programme, she asked him what families they had had so far.

'Oh, lots of 'em,' said Ken. 'Let me see, the Denhams, the Costas, the Murdochs ...'

'Oh,' she said, 'the *Iris* Murdochs?'

Ken didn't bat an eyelid.

'Well, actually, he calls himself Dickie,' he said.

Though the programme was largely based on general

knowledge questions, Kenneth delighted in slipping in the occasional trick ones like:

'What does a kitten become after it is three days old?'

Answer: 'Four days old.'

And when Warren Mitchell appeared in the show, Kenneth asked him:

'If you went into a Post Office, bought a stamp, and asked the assistant to stick it on a letter for you, and he refused, what would you do?'

Warren Mitchell got as far as: 'I'd stick it—', and then the roof fell in!

The England cricketer, Trevor Bailey, was asked:

'Who was the first Yorkshire captain to go to Australia?'

Bailey, terribly well read in the annals of cricket, pondered:

'Let me see,' he said. 'I think it must have been— Lord Hawke.'

Kenneth chortled with delight.

'Actually, it was Captain Cook. He was the son of a Yorkshire ploughman!'

Here is a splendid story Kenneth told against himself.

He had been compering an I.T.V. 'Give-away' Quiz for a long series, and each week when half-time arrived and the commercial was due, he always turned to the camera and said:

'That's all for the moment, we'll be back with you very shortly.'

One day he thought he'd be clever and change the routine, and, having just given away quite a lot of money to a dear old lady for answering three very simple questions, he ushered her off the stage and said to the viewers:

'There goes Mrs Moore proudly carrying in her hand thirty-seven pounds ten shillings. And now we're going to show her a very good way in which she can spend that money.'

The studio broke, and on to a monitor flashed the commercial.

It was exclusively devoted to Andrex toilet rolls!

'Top of the Form' covered a wide area of the country, visiting schools in every part of the British Isles.

A particularly successful session in 1966 came from Falkirk High School, and after the broadcast Kenneth was interviewed for the school magazine, who later printed the following piece.

SOLO FOR HORNE UNACCOMPANIED
(or almost)

The most popular person in Falkirk High School this year next to Primo and Illya Kuryakin, has been most definitely Mr Kenneth Horne. The magazine committee accept responsibility for the questions, but certainly not the answers.

Q. What school and/or university did you go to, and what effect did they have on your life? If none, say none.

A. St George's School, Harpenden (co-educational), London School of Economics, for one year, Magdalene College, Cambridge. Little—except that university life teaches you to live.

Q. Did you have any particular training for the job

you do, and what would be your advice to young
people who wanted to follow a career such as
yours—apart from 'DON'T'?

A. I had absolutely no training, but a great deal of
luck. Advice? Make quite certain you have a
second string to your bow.

Q. What sort of fan-mail do you get, and have you
had any letters which stand out in your memory?

A. Let's not call it 'fan-mail', just mail. I get about
twenty letters per day. 50% ask for autographs,
20% are complimentary, 10% are critical, 15%
ask me to open fetes or to do some charitable
deed, and 5% are just plain rude. And it's the
last category that one remembers.

Q. Is there a story behind the red carnation?

A. I've worn one every day since I was 21 (that's
about ten years). My father loved flowers. I think
a small splash of colour each day looks cheerful.
It's swank too.

Q. Paul McCartney said of Falkirk, 'A cemetery with
buses and taxis running through it'. What's your
opinion of Falkirk?

A. My knowledge of Falkirk is much too infinitesimal
to warrant any comment.

Q. When you were here, we were very impressed by
your unflappability but have you ever been really
embarrassed or put out when broadcasting?

A. Yes, but the stories are too long to tell, and
ought to be unsuitable for your high-class publication.

Q. Do you find that being in the public eye so much
limits your private life?

A. It's only by chance that one is in the public eye;
it's just earning one's living in the entertainment
field that limits one's private life.

Q. How are the scripts written for your radio show?
Are they spontaneous or the combined efforts of
many people?

A. Combined effort of Marty Feldman and Barry
Took, with a modest contribution of 'additional
material by K.H.', and some spontaneity during
the programme.

Q. Do recent trends in satire amuse or disgust you?

A. Glad you said recent trends; people think that
satire is new. Some satire amuses me; let's say that
some is just unsuitable for the medium in question.

Q. There's a lot said about the irresponsibility of
youth today. What do you think, keeping in mind
that on a programme such as 'Top of the Form',
you are meeting the elite of the school population?

A. I take the last sentence with a pinch of salt! I'm
not nearly so keen on the 'elite' as on the 'nice',
and it is the latter that I always come across on
'Top of the Form'. Much too much has been said
already about the irresponsibility of youth; it's
about time their P.R.O. clamped down.

Q. There is obviously a place in television for women
like Joan Clark, but why do you think there are
no women comperes, comedians or satirists?

A. You mean comediennes, commeres, satirettes.
Neither sex likes to hear a woman telling a joke
in public. I honestly don't know the answer to

women comperes. Personally, I like women an-
nouncers, but apparently the Great British Public
doesn't.

Q. If you were to write a book about yourself, what
would you call it?

A. Solo for Horne—Unaccompanied.*

Q. From your long repertoire of short stories, what's
the funniest you've ever been told?

A. That's unfair! They never sound funny on paper.

Q. Is there any truth in the rumour that you wear a
wig?

A. No, it's real skin.

Q. Would you be annoyed if your brand of humour
was called corny by today's standards?

A. Very little annoys me. Certainly not that.

Q. Do you have any pet hates apart from John
Ellison?

A. People who say 'Told you so!'

Q. If you had three wishes, what would you wish
for?

A. I've been pretty lucky in most things, so I think
all three would be for good health.

* I found 'Unaccompanied' cumbersome, and dropped it along the
way. N.H.

16 "little girls get bigger ..."

At the age of seventeen, Susan left St James's, Malvern, and went for a year to a finishing school in Switzerland. After this, she had a job with Marks & Spencer, which she seems to have enjoyed.

Kenneth's affection for her never diminished; and although he never interfered in the matter of her upbringing, he seems to have had a subtle influence over her to which she instinctively responded.

An instance of this is illustrated by an incident which happened shortly after her eighteenth birthday. She was working in Torquay. Kenneth had some professional engagement which brought him to the town, and was, as usual, installed in the Imperial Hotel. On the Saturday night he invited Susan, for a treat, to have dinner with him and stay the night.

At that time, she was rather pleased with herself and a bit of a show-off. She was determined to look sensational for this dinner, and in the splendour of her room at the Imperial she spent a great deal of time getting ready. She finally made her entrance into the bar where he was waiting for her. Her eyes were made-up with bright green eye-shadow extending up to her eyebrows which were heavily pencilled in black. The effect, to say the least, was striking. Kenneth took one look at her, grinned broadly, and said:

'I see. You're all ready for Faust, eh?'

She stopped in her tracks, turned tail, and retreated to her bedroom, where she wiped away a few tears with the offending make-up. Ten minutes later, she reappeared in the bar.

'Hello, darling,' he said. 'My goodness, how pretty you look!'

Sadly, there was always a tricky and highly fraught triangular relationship with Marjorie, to whom Kenneth maintained his totally committed loyalty, and even in the most trivial situation he would never take Susan's part against her. I think it says much for Susan's character that, in spite of this, even as she grew up, her devotion to him continued.

So, in 1960, she reached the age of twenty-one, which by any standards must be acknowledged as being grown-up.

In July of that year she went on holiday with her friend Susan Walker to a hotel in Majorca. It just so happened (and I suppose it comes under the heading of 'Fate') that a certain Mr Andrew Montague and his friend Mr Brian Carter had elected to take their holidays at precisely the same time, and were staying in the same hotel. It didn't take them all very long to get acquainted, though there was a slight problem at the end of the first evening, when the girls, comparing notes about the preliminary skirmish, each found that they preferred Mr Montague.

But Miss Thomas was a determined young woman,

and brought some pressure to bear by reminding Miss Walker of her involvement with a fairly steady gentleman friend back in England. So, for the honour of the old school, would Miss W. kindly belt up and lay off Mr Montague!

Meanwhile, in another part of the forest, the boys were weighing up the runners, and deciding, like perfect gentlemen, that the most sporting thing to do was to toss for it. Andy won, and opted for Susan Walker.

That evening they all went out to the local nightclub, and as the evening wore on, Andy realized that his two-headed penny for once had failed him, and, dammit, he'd picked the wrong girl! Bashing the Bacardi with slightly too reckless abandon, he suddenly realized he was fried to the gills, and must beat a hasty retreat. Returning some fifteen minutes later, minimally restored, he found his friend Brian locked in the arms of Susan Walker on the dance-floor, while Susan (T.) alone at the table was fighting off the local talent. This was a far more promising situation, and he quickly took advantage of it. By the end of the evening the relationship seems to have been amicably sorted out all round, and the rest of the holiday was an unqualified success. Andy and Susan by then had fallen deeply in love, and, back in England, continued to meet regularly. By November they had decided that they wanted to marry. Andy, intent upon doing the proper thing, called on Kenneth to ask his formal permission. Kenneth, while receiving him perfectly amiably, refused to be implicated: 'Nothing to do with me, dear boy, you'll have to ask her mother.'

"LITTLE GIRLS
   GET BIGGER..."

Susan had already asked her mother, and had not been sympathetically received. Marjorie had arbitrarily decided that she did not approve of Susan's choice. Pressed to state her objection Marjorie declared that he wasn't good enough for her. He was not, it is true, from the landed gentry, but he was a good-looking amiable young man from a good family, with some money inherited from his parents, who had died when he was a child; educated at Rugby and Magdalen College, Oxford. Andy and Susan were both annoyed and distressed at Marjorie's attitude. They were legally of age, and there was no cause or just impediment why they shouldn't marry. After some bitter arguments, with Marjorie insisting they should wait for at least a year, a compromise was struck, and they agreed to an engagement of nine months.

They were married on September 2nd, 1961, at Christ Church, Kensington, just around the corner from Cottesmore Court. Kenneth gave the bride away. Marjorie attended. The reception was at The Hyde Park Hotel.

One year later, in October 1962, Kenneth and Marjorie went for a holiday to Grenada, which seems to point to some kind of reconciliation. Lying on the beach, in blazing sunshine, Marjorie turned to him and asked:

'If you could have anyone here, sharing this holiday, whom would you most like?'

Who can say what passed through Kenneth's mind in the brief pause for reflection, before he replied:

'Susan. It would be nice for us all to be together again.'

Marjorie, too, was silent for a moment, before she said:

'All right. Why don't you ask her to come out? We've still got ten days.'

I cannot guess at who was kidding whom; what was going on in their minds, or whether they really thought about it at all. But Kenneth went straight into the hotel, and put a telephone call through to Susan in London.

Susan and Andy had been married for just about one year. They were blissfully happy, and still in that state of enchantment when every minute spent together is precious, and every one apart a privation. Andy had a job, and probably could not have gone anyway, but Kenneth neither invited him, nor even mentioned him. To Susan he said:

'I've booked you an air-ticket. Pick it up from the travel agency. We'd love you to come and join us for ten days.'

Susan said: 'But ... I don't think I can. Anyway, I'll have to ask Andy. I'll call you back tomorrow.'

She talked to Andy. With much unselfishness he said 'Of course you must go.'

So she went; and, after all, she could hardly fail to enjoy ten days in the sun in Grenada. But the incident left a scar in her mind which never quite healed.

I am convinced that Kenneth never had any personal animosity for Andy. There was not the remotest reason why he should have. But Marjorie was never reconciled; so here was the same insoluble problem. It must have distressed him, because he never bore ill-will, and to be forced into a position where he appeared to do just that would surely have been intolerable. But this was his greatest weakness. He shrank from resolving a situation where somebody had to get hurt; and let's face it, somebody always has to get hurt.

Susan's first child, a daughter Sarah, was born in March 1965 at The Middlesex Hospital in London. Marjorie and Kenneth came to see her and the new baby. Kenneth seemed subdued and rather embarrassed. Susan remained in the hospital for two weeks. Andy was fending for himself in a small furnished flat. Significantly, Marjorie and Kenneth never once invited him for a meal. In June, Sarah was christened at Christ Church, Kensington, and neither Marjorie nor Kenneth attended the christening. Susan was sad and disappointed, but rose above it.

Two years later, in 1967, their second daughter, Lisa, arrived. They were now living in Berkshire and in due course her christening was arranged at the parish church. Once again Marjorie declined to attend. Kenneth excused himself saying he had to be in Plymouth that day. Poor Susan wrote him a private letter:

'I am deeply hurt, and for the last time I am asking you please to come to Lisa's christening. Either make the effort, for me, or don't ever expect anything more from me again.'

He arrived at the church in a hire-car, in which he had been driven all the way from Plymouth. At the end of the service, he gave Susan a loving hug, got into the car and drove straight back. This seems to have been the start of the breakthrough, because, shortly afterwards, while on another visit to Plymouth, he invited Susan and Andy, who were on holiday in Cornwall, to meet

him. They both remember having supper with him in
the hotel, late one night after his show. Suddenly all
the barriers were down. Susan sat and marvelled as she
watched him talking easily to Andy in his old relaxed
manner. It was a new close relationship between the
three of them, and it continued for the rest of his life.

17 ad-vantage

I THINK the instant success of his full-time career in broadcasting probably did more to boost his morale, and so improve his health, than any medical treatment, although such treatment continued with great concentration. He was never really as well as he made out, but it was almost a matter of principle that he never discussed his health, apart from mostly assuring people that he 'felt fine', and, very rarely admitting to his closer friends that he was 'a bit second-hand today'. He never lost his limp after the stroke, but he devised a way of disguising it, which fooled most of the people. He found standing very tiring; yet, in his radio shows, when everyone always stood at the microphone, he did too, although he could easily have been seated at a separate microphone. Kenneth Williams has said that Ken always stood with his left arm on his shoulder, leaning fairly heavily. Few people realized that this support was a great help to him. He had his regular physiotherapy sessions with Joe, and a strict regimen of anti-coagulant drugs, which, it seems, was all that medical science could offer him. But his own best antidote was hard work, and as his radio and television reputation snowballed, so he began to work harder and harder.

He was in tremendous demand for television commercials, and at that time there were also programmes called Advertising Magazines (known in the trade as 'Admags'), which were fifteen to twenty minute blocks of advertising time, of which individual advertisers could buy up to three minutes each to demonstrate and hard sell any particular item of merchandise. These programmes were usually presented by a personality, assisted by a few demonstrators. One quite extraordinary regulation governing them, was that they must concentrate on advertising and have no preponderance of entertainment content! This, of course, is a clause in the Television Act, which totally prohibits the sponsoring of an entertainment programme by a named advertiser. This regulation gave rise to some fearful arguments and controversies. Just *when* are you being too entertaining in an Admag? I can well imagine that the majority of Kenneth's came perilously near breaching the Act! I need hardly say that it wasn't long before he realized that the best way to make a particular product stick in a viewer's mind is to make him laugh about it. It has twice the psychological impact of facing him deadpan and extolling its merits. Advertisers tend to take themselves far too seriously anyhow, and Kenneth had some considerable arguments in the early days, until he delivered an ultimatum which said, in effect: 'Either I do it my way, or I don't do it at all.'

I don't know how many Admags he did in various regions but there was one particular series which he made for Tyne Tees Television, in Newcastle, in 1960.

AD-VANTAGE

It was called 'Trader Horne' (he was always brilliant at titles!) and it ran for a total of thirty-six weeks every Sunday afternoon, until the Independent Television Authority clamped down on the whole lovely racket.

Graham Tennant was then, and still is, the managing director of a prominent commercial stationers and office equipment company in Darlington. He was also a part-time radio actor in North Regional programmes, with a lot of broadcasting experience, and a fully paid-up member of Equity. When Kenneth embarked upon this programme he invented a character whom he called 'Mr Stallibrass', who was to have a regional accent, and act as one of the demonstrators of the products. Graham Tennant was invited by Tyne Tees to audition for the job, which he got. 'Mr Stallibrass' turned out to be another 'Edward Wilkinson' creation, and Graham was constantly receiving letters from numerous members of the Stallibrass family, enquiring as to their possible relationship!

Apart from Graham, the team was composed of Kenneth, as the main presenter, and actress Ann Croft as the other demonstrator. Joyce Davis wrote the scripts and liaised with the various advertising agencies concerned.

Kenneth, Ann and Joyce travelled each Friday to Newcastle, where they met up with Graham at the studio, and recorded the programme for the following Sunday. Ann Croft remembers those rail journeys. They used to play 'Consequences'; but, in Kenneth's game of 'Consequences', every contribution had to rhyme with the previous line, which made it just that bit harder, and funnier.

One week there was a strike of railway buffet staff, so no food was available on the trains. This didn't matter so much on the journey north, but presented more of a problem on the way back. The train time-tables were pretty tight, and they only ever just made the fast train, after the recording, with minutes to spare, which left no time to eat before the journey. They shrugged it off. Just one of those things. Have to go hungry till we get home! But, as they arrived at the train for the return journey, they were met by three white-coated waiters from The Royal Station Hotel, Newcastle. They produced three hampers, ordered by Mr Kenneth Horne, which they loaded into the dining-car. The first contained champagne, whisky, gin and mineral waters. The second, two cold chickens, rolls and butter. The third? Sandwiches; emergency rations for such passengers who, ignorant of the strike, might venture along to the dining-car in search of refreshment. They ended up with some twenty people in the dining-car, playing charades, and having a ball!

At the end of the series, Kenneth wanted to arrange a celebration dinner for all the artists and production staff, but it became too difficult with people having to get home afterwards. So, instead, he promoted a gala breakfast party at nine o'clock on the morning of the last recording, with champagne and oysters and every imaginable goodie. I am only sorry I never saw the programme they made after it! Graham Tennant expressed the feelings of everybody connected with this happy venture, when he wrote:

'Kindness, charm, good humour, generosity; these were Kenneth Horne's attributes and we all loved him.

AD-VANTAGE

I always look upon it as a rather special part of my life; and perhaps the best tribute I can pay is to say that I feel a glow of pride and warm well-being to be able to say "I knew Kenneth Horne".'

Joyce continued to work with Kenneth as P.A. on his radio and television shows throughout the year 1960. In particular she was concerned with a show for Southern Television called 'Snakes and Ladders'. This was an audience participation show, for which she interviewed and selected from a large number of applicants the contestants to take part in each programme. The programmes were outside broadcasts from various locations in the Southern area.

During the summer the programme was visiting Eastbourne, and Joyce, looking through the local newspaper, drew Kenneth's attention to an advertisement for a period flint built thatched cottage in the village of Alciston, which lies on the far side of the South Downs some eight miles from Eastbourne. Kenneth was always a man of immediate action if anything appealed to him, and, in the first possible break from the preparation of the programme, they went together to the agents, picked up the key, and drove out to see the cottage. He fell in love with it at sight. It was exactly what he had been dreaming about for the past two years. His dream, in fact, had gone rather further than this, for what he really wanted was for Joyce to share it with him. For they were still devoted to each other.

By now, of course, Marjorie knew. Some 'well-wisher' had seen to that. But divorce was something she refused to consider. It could fairly be said that she had never worked very hard at holding their marriage together, but neither was she generous enough to let it drift amicably apart. Rather melodramatically, she threatened suicide if he even thought of leaving her. Close friends, who knew, were liberal with their advice and conflicting opinions. It was ever thus. But, in the final issue, there was really only one person who had to take the initiative, and resolution was never his strongest suit.

The news of this drama, naturally enough, reached his family, who were somewhat appalled. They seemed to think that the scandal of a divorce, or even a separation, would ruin Kenneth's career. With respect, I venture to suggest that they were probably mistaken; even though, perhaps, it is impertinent to take sides in a matter as intensely personal as this.

Poor old chum, he had certainly made a fairly spectacular lash-up of his matrimonial life over the previous thirty years! I think it might be said of him that he was forever in love with being in love, and one wonders whether any marriage would ever have succeeded for him on a permanent basis? He bought 'Sturtles', for that was the name of the dream-cottage, and for the next eight years he spent almost all his free time there, very often with Marjorie, though sometimes alone.

In November 1960, Joyce, not surprisingly, had a nervous breakdown, and the following year, through her own unaided efforts (contrary to some reports!), she got herself a very good job in Germany. This might be said to have been the end of the affair—except that, for her, it never ended.

For Kenneth, work became the only anodyne; he took on more and more. One of the shows which he joined in 1961 as permanent chairman was 'Twenty Questions', which he lifted to a new peak. Never was this programme better, in the whole of its long history, than during the eight years we had with Kenneth; and, for me, never was it quite as stimulating and enjoyable, particularly from 1965 when I joined the panel and worked more closely with him.

It was in these years that my wife, Pam, and I initiated the annual 'Twenty Questions' tea-party. One of our regular outside broadcasts each year always took place from The Leas Cliff Hall, Folkestone. Our house is some thirty miles from Folkestone, and could scarcely be said to lie on the direct route from London. But it seemed as good an opportunity as any of entertaining our chums, who kindly made the slight detour on their journey from London, and arrived in time for a socking tea with strawberries and cream, which, hopefully, we would arrange in the garden.

In 1968, we had constructed in the garden a small ornamental pond, some fifteen feet long by about seven feet wide. For a joke, when sending out the invitations, I wrote:

'Mr and Mrs Norman Hackforth request the pleasure of the company of Mr Kenneth Horne on Wednesday, August 7th, 1968, at 3.00 p.m. Tea by the lake.'

Kenneth replied (and I treasure it still):

'Kenneth Horne intends to be at Honeysuckle Cottage soon after 3.00 p.m. on August 7th, and will bring bathing costume (with straps). Kenneth Horne says that the Hackforths are very kind people. Kenneth Horne says that Pam is the prettier of the two.'

18 funny girl

ONCE upon a time, many years ago (in 1952), there were three little girls, aged fourteen, who were pupils at Rochester Grammar School. They listened avidly to every single broadcast of 'Much-Binding-in-the-Marsh', and every single repeat. They couldn't even wait a whole week for the next programme, so one of them, whose name was Mollie Sharp, used to write bits of the script in advance, in the authentic Horne and Murdoch idiom, and the trio would perform these together secretly in a corner of the gymnasium on wet days.

Finally Mollie was dared by her friends to send some of her original material to Kenneth and Dickie. She picked out the best bits and put them together. She wrote a covering letter, and addressed it to Kenneth at his private address, which precociously she had discovered. As she dropped the letter into the pillar-box her knees turned to jelly. Not even her parents knew of this audacious act, only her two friends who were sworn to secrecy. She adopted the pen-name of Mollie Bernard. She waited in trepidation, and in due course came a reply :

'Dear Miss Bernard,

Thank you very much for your letter, and for the material which you enclosed. I have shown this to Richard Murdoch and we both agree that it is very promising. We shall hope to use some of your ideas in forthcoming programmes of "Much-Binding-in-the-Marsh", and I enclose a cheque as an advance payment, which I hope you will find satisfactory. If you would like to come to a broadcast, perhaps you would contact my secretary, Miss Davis, who will be pleased to arrange to send you tickets.

Yours sincerely,
Kenneth Horne.'

Mollie nearly fainted! She got the precious tickets, and the following week the three of them turned up at The Paris studio, where, spellbound, they watched their idols perform. Afterwards they actually met them. Recalling this historic meeting, some twenty-three years later, Mollie told me:

'When you have built up a mental picture of someone whom you have admired tremendously, it wouldn't have been surprising if meeting them for the first time didn't turn out to be a bit of a disappointment. But, far from this, he turned out to be even nicer than I had ever dreamed.'

I don't doubt that Ken and Dickie goggled a bit to find that their promising script-writer was barely fifteen years old. But there was no denying the fact that she had a definite aptitude for comedy writing, and, what is more, for the particular type of wacky humour upon which 'Much-Binding' was built.

Mollie contributed quite a number of ideas over the next two years, which they used in the scripts and paid her for. Then, in 1954, 'Much-Binding' finally came to an end.

Little Miss Sharp had other things to occupy her life, other big decisions to make. Her parents had always been members of the Salvation Army, which she too had joined as a child, and continued to work for.

At the age of eighteen, she met and fell in love with a young man named Daniel Millest. He was a full-time officer in the Salvation Army, with the rank of captain, which may perhaps have influenced Mollie's decision that she too would dedicate her life to the same cause.

They married in 1958, and worked together. It is scarcely the most lucrative career. There is never very much over to put away for that proverbial rainy day.

In 1960, when they already had two sons, Dan met with an accident which injured his spine, and left him totally incapacitated and unable to work. After a while it became clear that he would not be able to continue with his work in 'The Army', and, since Mollie had to look after him, they both resigned.

Times were a bit hard. They were living on National Assistance in a small house in Derby, which had no electricity. They somehow acquired a transistor radio, and one of the first programmes Mollie tuned in to was 'Beyond our Ken'.

She wrote to Kenneth and filled in some of the gaps in the past six years, and of course he wrote back:

'Dear Mollie,

I am indeed sorry to hear of your husband's accident and illness. I have tremendous sympathy with him

because, three years ago I had a stroke, which means I
shall never again be able to get the normal enjoyment
out of life. However, we're lucky to be alive! One thing
that you, of all people, need not worry about is the
financial future. With your talent for writing, I would
take a bet that it won't be very long before you are
earning very good money.

Now then. As far as "B.O.K." goes the position is
rather delicate! Our script-writer is very temperamental, and often fails to clock in with a script in time,
with the result that K.H. has to do a last minute job.

I would love you to submit a few jottings, because I
have a feeling that in the next series (starting in September) I shall be increasingly called upon to help. In
that case we'll put the whole thing on a proper financial
basis. Meanwhile, there will be lots of other script-
writing opportunities, and you have my assurance that
I'll see you get one of them.

I look forward to hearing from you again.

All the best,

Kenneth Horne.'

So she started again, and wrote for him for the next
seven years.

Had anyone ever asked me: 'Where does Kenneth
Horne get all those wonderful jokes from?', it would
not have occurred to me to reply: 'Oh, didn't you
know? A lady in the Salvation Army writes them for
him!' But I would have been marginally right. Mollie
did not, of course, write all those wonderfully funny
jokes. But she did have a quite uncanny facility for
slanting ideas which Kenneth was able to use. Precisely

what he wrote and what Mollie wrote would be hard to separate, and remember too that there were some very expert professional writers involved as well. But, from the hundred odd letters which Mollie has shown me, it is quite evident that here were two lively inventive minds, each with a similar and complementary sense of the ridiculous, and they successfully struck sparks off each other.

There were occasions, of course, when she quite straightforwardly ghosted pieces which appeared under his name, though he probably crossed the t's and dotted the i's, and without his name the pieces would hardly have seen the light of day.

He was kindly critical at times, as for example in one letter:

'Too many puns. Too many old gags. Maybe you *think* you've invented them!'

But he was unfailingly encouraging, and unstinting with praise and appreciation when she got it right. All the time he fired ideas at her:

'I've got three TV Agricultural Show Admags to do. Most of the content is hard advertising, but I am allowed about two and a half minutes out of the fifteen as linking-material. Any agricultural whimsicalities, or Mollieisms which I could fit in anywhere?'

In 1963, Mollie asked him if he would appear at a Salvation Army rally in Derby, and he agreed. In a letter confirming arrangements he wrote:

'One thing I meant to ask you. Is this "do" a very serious affair? Is it in a place in which laughter is frowned upon? It would be bad if I were to paralyse everyone with clean witticisms, and then have to say:

"And now we will sing four choruses of Fight the Good Fight". Or is the whole affair a pleasant unreligious (as opposed to irreligious) concert?

'By the way, if absolutely necessary I shall have to come up on the train reaching Derby at 4.35. My point yesterday was that, in the normal way, an artist hates getting to a show a minute before he has to. You see, one is much better and fresher without having to meet a lot of people before hand. That is the dread of entertainers, and the most tiring part of all! So, if I'm not really wanted, then I can reach Derby at 6.42? Marvellous!

K.'

Mollie said: 'He was a riotous success, of course. He told us dozens of unlikely but funny stories; he told us about his work; he told us about his father, and he sang, and joined in with us. His presence was a joy to us, and he told us that he enjoyed every second as much as we did.'

Later the same year, discussing pet-hates as a possible programme idea, he wrote:

'I hate people talking about someone who has "passed-on" or "passed over", or "been taken". How do they know whether someone has passed "on, backwards, forwards or sideways"? The simple answer is they're dead! Also, why are people suddenly referred to as "poor" when they die?'

She took it all in her stride, in the midst of looking after Dan (who, happily, eventually got better and was able to work again), raising three fine sons, and selflessly devoting a large part of her life to the Salvation Army, of which she has remained a member. Of Kenneth, she says:

'He was my fan-club of one!'

A very remarkable lady, Mrs Mollie Millest.

19 initial success

I T is quite a feat, juggling with the story of Kenneth's life, to keep all the balls in the air at the same time. He had so many projects that I fear it is inevitable that some of them must get crowded out.

As far as his activities in radio and television are concerned, in the fifties and sixties alone he appeared in no less than fifty different named programmes, many of which I must confess I had never even heard of. I suppose one of the reasons for his tremendous success was that he never turned down any job which he could, by any physical possibility, manage to fit in, provided the idea of it appealed to him. More than once I heard him say:

'If I don't like doing something, I don't bloody well do it!' But do not be misled by this remark. I can't believe that he always 'liked' travelling many hundreds of miles to take part, with no financial reward, in some charitable enterprise. But if he liked the person who asked him, or he liked the whole idea, then that was enough.

He seldom argued about money. He enjoyed every minute of his life as a performer, and he said of him-

self: 'I am the highest-paid amateur in the business.'
This was one of the grossest misstatements of fact.
Firstly, anyone less amateurish, with such a high professional expert approach to his work would have been
hard to find. Secondly, he was by no means highly
paid. He was in the happy position of being able to do
a great deal of work, and thereby earn a great deal of
money.

Pat Newman, for many years Booking Manager of
the B.B.C. Drama and Light Entertainment Department, Radio (or, with the Corporation's passion for
initials, B.M.D.L.E.R.), told me that Kenneth was the
very favourite artist with whom that department ever
had dealings. In the first place, he handled his own
business without employing an agent, whose main pur-
pose in life, naturally enough, is forever striving to
bump up the fees, and so, his own commission. Thus
the department was saved the endless boredom of having to argue the toss. Secondly, Kenneth himself seemed
happy to accept without argument whatever fee was
offered. As the years went by, and his success rocketed,
this became almost embarrassing. So Pat was delighted
when one day one of his assistants came to his office,
and said with some concern:

'Oh Mr Newman, I have just been talking to Mr
Kenneth Horne about a booking in this programme. I
mentioned the usual fee, and he says he thinks it should
be worth an extra five guineas.'

Pat's face beamed. 'Then for God's sake, let's give it
to him!'

He was once invited to appear as a guest in a serious
current affairs programme, involving a fair amount of

preparation. There seemed to be no precedent upon which Bookings could base the offer of a fee. Pat himself rang Kenneth, and the whole matter was amicably agreed without fuss. The contract was prepared, sent to Kenneth for signature, duly returned, and forwarded for payment in the customary way. Two days after the programme had actually taken place, Pat received a memo from a very exalted senior executive of the Corporation (whom, even after all those years have passed, and Pat now cosily in retirement, he declines to name for me!). The memo said, in effect, that it had come to the notice of this very exalted senior executive (V.E.S.E.) that, in the matter of an important current affairs programme recently transmitted, Mr Kenneth Horne's fee had been less than adequate. Would Mr Newman therefore arrange to pay to Mr Horne an extra twenty guineas in respect of his services on this programme.

Pat replied that, while appreciating V.E.S.E.'s point of view, the contract for this engagement had been signed by Mr Horne, and passed forward for processing, and it was now impossible to do anything more about it.

In due course a second memo from V.E.S.E. arrived on Pat's desk, stating, somewhat tetchily, that the previous memo had not been in the nature of a suggestion, but a firm directive, and would Mr Newman kindly act upon it forthwith.

Pat replied that he did not consider himself empowered to take the action which V.E.S.E. was demanding, and that he had passed the correspondence to his immediate superior for attention.

Pat's Immediate Superior (P.I.S.) upheld him; and, after some further somewhat tight-lipped discussion, it was agreed that the contract must stand.

Pat now got on the telephone to Kenneth:

'Ken, it's Pat Newman. About your current affairs broadcast last week. I had a memo from ... [V.E.S.E.!] saying we ought to give you an extra twenty guineas.'

'Jolly good, old boy! Thanks very much.'

'But you're not going to get it.'

'Oh! Aren't I? Too bad. Never mind. That was the quickest twenty guineas I never had.'

'Look, I can't tell you about it now; but it's a long time since we met, let me take you out to lunch one day next week. How about Tuesday? One o'clock at The Caprice?'

'Fine. I'll look forward to it.'

It should be pointed out that Pat, in his official capacity, was permitted to claim reasonable expenses for hospitality and entertainment for VIP artists.

They met as arranged; and, seated at the table, the waiter presented two outsize menus.

'Now!' said Pat. 'Never mind the bloody table d'hote, have a good look at the best of the à la carte dishes, because you're not getting up from this table until you've eaten twenty quid's worth of lunch!'

A final comment on the 'initial syndrome', in which Kenneth delighted, is illustrated in a memo he once sent to Barry Took which read:

INITIAL SUCCESS

TOP SECRET. NOT TO BE READ BY ANYONE.
INTERDEPARTMENTAL MEMORANDUM.

FROM: K. PUBES. (O.O.T.I.W.E.F.E.R.T.H.)
(One of those involved with every-
body's entertainment The Clitheroe
Kid.)

TO: A.C.W.E.F.E.R.T.H. (All concerned
with Everybody's favourite entertainment 'From Mantovani and Back',
with The Dennis Morris Dancers, accompanied by Les Bean on Pubes.)

RE: V.H.F. and F.M. (Veritable hip-flask,
and faintly medicinal)

KENNETH: (Sings to tune of 'I'm just a West Hart-
lepools Cabinet Pud', from The
Merry Window by Johann Sebastian
Perkins.)

Let's all drink from the hip-flask
Silver and shining and bright.
Let's all sample the Marc de Bour-
goyne
Till all our loose women are tight.

Let's discover if Newington Butts
And if so have butter for tea
    (N.B. A weak line. B.T. & M.F.)
Then see you return
All the Marc de Boy-gurne.,
And that glorious hip-flask to me.

(You are all *very* kind.)

20 correspondence course

Q u i t e early on in the first draft of this book, I wrote a sentence which read:

'I cannot believe that ever in his life did he experience loneliness, for he was a gregarious man with an enormous natural magnetism and a facility for making friends.'

Now, some months later, in the course of which I have met and talked to a great many people and stripped off several layers from this remarkably complex character, I have realized how mistaken I was. For, in the midst of an abundant life, bursting at the seams with activity and people, there is no doubt in my mind that Kenneth remained a lonely man. A man with a core of loneliness within himself, and a natural affinity when he recognized it in others.

Which perhaps explains the remarkable relationship which sprang up when he came across a certain lonely woman. Her name is Christine Bennett. She has quite freely allowed me to use her name, and she has also generously given me access to more than sixty treasured letters which she received between 1965 and 1968, from Kenneth Horne.

CORRESPONDENCE
COURSE

Christine would not want me to over-stress or drama-tize her life, but, briefly:

She married Geoffrey Bennett in 1946, and for eight years they were intensely happy. In 1954 he contracted pulmonary tuberculosis. He spent a year in hospital, and was finally discharged with rather less than half of one lung. He survived, miraculously, for another eight years, and died in 1963.

She was pretty low for the next eighteen months, which I think is an understatement. She had a job, which she never particularly enjoyed, and she com-muted for four hours a day.

Her greatest solace and recreation was the radio; and her very favourite performer, head and shoulders above all the rest, Kenneth Horne.

He was doing a 'Housewives Choice'; she wrote in with a request for a record, and, in reply, came letter number one, which simply said:

'Dear Mrs Bennett,

Thank you for your charming letter. I shall make a point of listening to Schubert's Erl King, and see if I can fit it into a programme.

Yours sincerely,

Kenneth Horne.'

He had probably written another twenty like that, the same day. He played her record in a programme, and she wrote to thank him. And so began this remark-able correspondence which continued regularly for the next four years.

I have never, of course, seen any of Christine's let-ters, but I am sure they were exceptional. Kenneth re-plied joyfully to every one. They are perfectly ordinary

CORRESPONDENCE COURSE

accounts of his day-to-day life, written mostly on train journeys. Gradually the letters become less formal. From 'Mrs Bennett', she becomes 'Dear Christine Bennett', and then 'Dear Christine', until he signs himself 'Love, Kenneth'. But, quite clearly, never did they come anywhere near to being 'love-letters', and never did this strange sincere friendship which blossomed ever get out of control.

She chatted away in her letters about events in her own life, for which she apologized as being pretty dull compared with his. She told him about her flat, in which she took pride, and in reply he wrote her a typical Ken Horne poem, witty and apposite:

> *I find it a time-passing dodge*
> *To try and imagine Park Lodge.*
> *Of course it's especially fun*
> *To conjure up Flat Number One.*
>
> *Does the sitting-room glisten like new?*
> *And has it a fabulous view?*
> *And is the settee*
> *As a settee* should *be,*
> *To seat (rather close) only two?*
>
> *Is the kitchen of modern design*
> *With a table at which one can dine?*
> *Do the cupboards conceal*
> *Everything for a meal*
> *Plus those neat little racks for the wine?*

CORRESPONDENCE COURSE

And now for the bedroom—oh dear!
I mustn't be too nosey here!
Silken sheets—and between
Lies the owner Christine—
Close your eyes, Horne, and then disappear!

I find for a poet like I'm
Christine is quite easy to rhyme.
But as for that other name, Bennett,
Well, that's quite impossible, 'ennit?

(Longfellow.)

She met him, in due course. She made a point of going to his broadcasts when she could.

One wet Saturday morning, returning from shopping, neither looking nor feeling her best, the telephone rang, and a voice which needed no identification said:

'I could be at your flat in two minutes, if it's all right with you.'

She nearly fainted! She rushed round the flat like a whirlwind, knocking it into shape. Drinks? All she had was a bottle of Dubonnet Blonde, then quite recently marketed. He arrived. He praised the flat. No, he'd never tried Dubonnet Blonde. H'm, delicious! He must make a note of it.

They talked. Above all, of course, they laughed. That's all.

When it was time for him to go:

'Walk to the car with me.'

'Are you sure that's all right?'

'Of course. Why shouldn't it be?'

CORRESPONDENCE
COURSE

It was the Bentley. KH6 number two. She admired it. Slightly overawed, she heard herself saying, with desperate banality:

'What's it like to be a celebrity?'

He grinned. 'D'you know, it's really rather fun!'

There is nothing in the letters which needed to be suppressed. Every word could have been published, except that the repetition of his travels, collectively, would have been slightly tedious. So here are a few selected extracts:

One of the earlier letters, dated October 29th, 1965, strangely shows another parallel with his father's medical history: 'For the first time in my life, I've had to cancel a broadcast. Something happened to my inside a few days ago, which absolutely doubled me up. The medicos think it's probably something to do with the kidneys, maybe a stone, but we await the result of an X-ray, which hasn't been taken yet!'

But on November 13th he was able to write: 'Apparently the X-rays are O.K., though they showed that something has recently been wandering over the kidney!'

November 19th, 1965: 'Next week is comparatively peaceful. Sleeper to Falkirk Monday night, back 10.00 p.m. Tuesday. Broadcast Wednesday, with a speech at an insurance dinner in the evening. Thursday is Plymouth day, which means I'm back about midday Friday. Saturday is free, then I have a big broadcast on Sunday.'

Continental Hotel, Plymouth, November 25th, 1965: 'It's about 4.30 p.m., and I've just had my cup of char after doing the first of my TV shows, two every

CORRESPONDENCE
COURSE

other Thursday. It went fairly well, though a little on the quiet side. There's a lot of interviewing to do, and people tend to go blank when the actual show starts. However, maybe tonight's epic will be gayer. Next Monday I shall be down at Southampton discussing a regular Sunday programme that they want me to do in the New Year. All very serious (I think) music and discussion, sort of 6-6.30-ish. Tuesday is "Top of the Form" (penultimate in the series) but luckily my team happens to be in Dulwich. Poor John Ellison has to go to South Wales! Wednesday I have a midday show, and spend the afternoon at the TV studios at Lime Grove. Thursday sees me doing TV in Newcastle again, and then I have three days off (what's gone wrong?).

'You'll be glad to hear that the insurance dinner went like a bomb, mainly because mine was the final speech, and they'd had to sit through four rather boring ones—so anything I said was rather a relief.

'Falkirk was fun. I arrived there in the wind and the rain, but by early afternoon the skies were clear and the sun was shining, so I decided to fly back instead of training it. Incidentally, my team won, so they're now in the final, and will meet the winners of Dulwich versus Maestog.

'Yes, Christmas is frighteningly near, and I'm already doing recordings of Christmas programmes, and of course I've just finished my *February* article for *She*!

'Christmas will not be over busy for me, and I'm trying to take the whole week after off, because once January starts I become even busier than I am now. No, I haven't had a proper holiday this year. In this business you only take a holiday if you're not working!

CORRESPONDENCE COURSE

I really only do Radio and TV these days, because the old left leg doesn't permit much youthful exuberance.'

The Sunday programme he was discussing turned out to be a fairly light-hearted religious TV show, presented by Southern Television the following year, which was called 'Heavens Above', and was scripted by Mollie Millest.

Interviewed about the programme, Kenneth said:

'This is religion given a completely human treatment. I loved the idea right from the start. Being the son of a clergyman I think anything that makes religion sound more real to the average person is a good idea. We are just trying to make people think a bit, in an entertaining way. I have had a tremendous lot of fun doing this programme. If you cannot enjoy religion, then I don't think there is much point in having it. I was only seven when my father died but my impression is of a man who liked his religion to be joyful. He didn't mind if people had a jolly good giggle in his church, and I am sure this is the sort of programme he would have loved. I have no doubt he would thoroughly have approved of religious programmes on television. He was a great orator, a little bit of a Billy Graham in his way. I think he would have shaken things up a bit if he had lived to appear on television.'

In the train, en route for Plymouth, May 12th, 1966: 'The carriage reeks of melon, because I have brought three Charentan melons with me, as I'm taking my producer and his wife out to a meal this evening, and the Plymouth melons are getting a bit long in the tooth.'

On May 24th, 1966 he wrote: 'Have been spending

the last few days trying to write a one-off radio show
for myself and Ken Williams, which I am thinking of
calling "Twice Ken is Plenty".'

Once again, this title was one of Mollie Millest's in-
ventions. He had written to her on April 5th, 1966: 'I
can't help feeling that a Ken H and Ken W show might
be a riot. And by Ken H and Ken W I mean just that.
No one else histrionically speaking. "The Two Kens?"
—"D'ye ken Ken?" Would you like to turn this over
in your mind and then drop me a note?'

Mollie wrote to him with the 'Twice Ken is Plenty'
suggestion, to which he replied on May 17th, 1966:
'Sounds fine to me. I'll work on it.'

By June 9th he wrote to Christine: 'My epic has
slowed down a bit and I'm doing a bit of re-writing.
The trouble is that with my sort of script the more you
read it the less funny it seems!'

And on the 11th, to Mollie:

'Re "Twice Ken—". No. I have made no progress
and I think you and I should have a chat.'

They eventually got out a specimen script, which
Kenneth took to producer Humphrey Barclay. Sadly
it wasn't funny enough, and on August 25th came a
letter from Humphrey, of which Kenneth sent a copy
to Mollie:

'My dear Kenneth,

I'm sorry to say I have failed with "Twice Ken
is Plenty".

This will be disappointing to you as it is surprising
to me. I really thought we'd get a chance to do it, but
a definite "No" has come this morning ... I'm sorry

we won't be working on it, I was looking forward to
that very much.'

Even Ken couldn't win 'em all!

I am quite certain that Humphrey's disappointment
was genuine. He would have jumped at the chance of
working again with Kenneth, for his association with
him over 'Twenty Questions' had been one of his
happiest and most rewarding times, as this brief appreciation confirms:

'I loved working with him. He was kindness itself to
the neophyte me, and made me feel much more important than I was throughout my two years. Our office
sessions trying to think up the objects were hilarious;
nothing was ever less like work. We spent most of the
time falling about with laughter, and only just used
to emerge at the end of the session with a more or less
sensible list, though with Kenneth on the job you'd
never stop the occasional devilment creeping in, like
"TEASTED TOE-CAKE"! But he was of course so
conscientious, and how he found the time to spend
those joyful mornings with me I'll never know.

'I was so fond of him, and proud to be his producer;
and was helped enormously by his generosity, gentility,
and sense of fun and proportion.'

Two more light-hearted letters of Kenneth's that
year: 'Among the lighter tasks today is an article for
Woman's Hour on train-cum-car ferries in the U.K.
Fascinating! And so *sexy*!'

'I'm not a great lover of things that smack of the
medical in a magazine like *She*, and I am constantly
remarking about this, much to the amusement of the
Editor. She knows that apparently women lap these

things up, and adore being medically frightened.'

And then quite a gap in the correspondence, explained in his letter dated January 21st, 1967:

'This really is about the first letter I have written to anyone since having had a rather sharp heart attack on October 5th last. I had five and a half weeks in bed, and then a period of convalescence till the end of the first week in January, when the medicos said I could re-start work on a gentle scale. Unfortunately the day I started I managed to collect a monumental cold and throat which is only now leaving me. Rather naturally I feel more second-hand than I should.

'I shall never be able to undertake a full schedule, as the heart apparently now has a permanent "murmur", and everything has to be done at a slow pace. However, things might be worse (as they say!).'

And again, in April, he wrote:

'You ask kindly after me. Well, I suppose you might say that I bought rather a packet last October. I returned after three months, but I think that was really about a month too soon.

'In any event, continued headaches etc., made the experts think that the blood was too rich(!) So 24 hours in Bart's where they kept taking blood away and putting it back. Eventually a gentleman called Bodley Scott (who apparently looks after the Queen so *should* be OK!) said things weren't as bad as he'd expected! The arteries were not rock-hard, but a good deal less pliable than they should be. No injections therefore, just pills to thin the blood and (I'm told) calm the nerves!

'What the future holds, no one really knows, but I

think that two shows a week are enough for a man of my advanced years!

'I've just read this. It sounds a bit depressing. It's not meant to be, I'm not like that.'

I don't think any of his radio colleagues knew about this. I certainly did not. He came back for that year's series of 'Twenty Questions' as bright and vigorous as ever; and I was interested to find that on October 16th he wrote:

'This week I am guesting in something called "The Tennis-Elbow-Foot Game" with my old chum Norman Hackforth. Such is fame!'

The rest of the Christine Bennett correspondence belongs later in this book.

21 pavane

FRIDAY, February 14th, 1969 is one of those dates which are indelibly imprinted in my memory.

In the first place, it happened to be my twentieth wedding anniversary. Second, when I woke in the morning and tried to leave my bed, I let out a shout of agony and found myself totally locked and unable to move, due to what I then called lumbago, but subsequently turned out to be rather more permanently spinal osteo-arthritis.

Any plans we may have had by way of modest celebration throughout the day were clearly cancelled, for having been gently eased back into my bed I could only hope to remain prostrate for at least the following twenty-four hours.

In the evening, my darling wife produced an epicurean dinner on a table at my bedside, with a splendid bottle of claret, after which, though still immobilized, I felt considerably better.

All of which explains how it came about that, at no time that evening, did we switch on the television.

The first thing I remember on waking the following day was the newspapers landing on my bed as Pammie brought my breakfast. I picked up the *Daily Express*, and caught sight of the aggressive black letters of that fearful headline:

'DRAMA AS KENNETH HORNE DIES'

In case you don't remember; he had been announcing the award winners at the annual Guild of Television Producers presentation party at the Dorchester Hotel. The ceremony, in a ballroom packed with show-biz names, was being tele-recorded for later transmission. He was, they said, at the top of his form, the audience roaring with laughter, when, quite suddenly, he swayed forward and fell off the platform.

It was reported that Lord Hill, then Chairman of the B.B.C. Governors, gave him the kiss of life. I don't know why this should strike me as a fearful, macabre joke. I just know, beyond any doubt, that Ken would have split his sides laughing.

They took him in an ambulance to St Georges Hospital. He was dead. So the last conscious moment he ever knew was the sweetest music of all. Great shouts of laughter.

I was just one of probably millions who mourned him that day. And yet one knew one must not weep for this great-hearted giant of humour. He wouldn't want our tears. He would want only our remembrance of his unquenchable laughter.

And, what a way to go! When the pain of the first shock had abated a little, one could only thank God for that. I pondered for a moment on how it *could* have been, had this final stroke not been instantly lethal. Can you imagine the sheer horror and indignity of him surviving, as a drooling paralysed cripple, for maybe several years? Oh no. This was never for 'Our Ken'.

PAVANE

He died the way he had always lived; with panache and dignity, right at the top.

I have his letters to Christine Bennett during the last full year of his life, which show more accurately than anything the pattern of his general condition during that year, of which few people were aware. Starting on December 12th, 1967, he wrote:

'Yes, "fair" is a pretty good description at the moment. I think the trouble is all these so-and-so pills that I have to take to keep the blood-pressure fairly steady, and the blood flowing at roughly the right rate. Whatever the reason, it is more than a bit of a nuisance, but I suppose I'm lucky, just the same.'

In February 1968 he wrote: 'However, here we are, getting a little bit more tired each time one has to broadcast, but still in one piece.'

Later, in July 1968: 'I haven't really had a holiday as yet, so the health remains much as before, and a little uncertain at that. On the other hand I am always better when I'm working so where does one go from there? At the moment I have 20Q's and a TV affair called "Horne-a-Plenty", which means three days rather exhausting rehearsal. But I have only one more to do. Being a bit of a 'name-dropper', I must tell you that on Wednesday I am speaking immediately after H.R.H. the D of E at a Guildhall dinner! Such is fame!'

He did not take any holiday that year, though a week later he wrote to Christine:

'I'm just off for two weeks at a Health Farm. I'm hoping that a good de-coke may help me back to a more certain life. I suppose my friends won't recognize me less $1\frac{1}{2}$ stone?'

This was entirely his own idea, and not his doctor's
or Joe Friel's. Joe says he could ill-afford to lose weight
at this time, but it was all a part of his determined fight
to get back to health. With hindsight, it seems clear
that he was chronically unwell during that year, though
meeting him, one would never have known it. Only
two months earlier, in June, I had asked him to help
me out, and he had gladly agreed without demur.

It was the time I was negotiating to get my radio
show, 'The Tennis-Elbow-Foot-Game' on to television,
and it was a bit of a struggle. I had finally managed to
arrange for a pilot tele-recording of the show on June
15th, and at the last moment Max Robertson, who was
chairman of the show, was prevented by an O.B. engagement abroad from doing the recording. To cancel
the date was too chancey; everybody else on the team
was booked. I telephoned Kenneth and told him the
situation. Would he come and stand in for Max that
day?

'Of course, dear boy, with pleasure. But I don't
know much about the game. Perhaps we could get together for an hour or two, so that you can brief me?'

He drove over from Alciston to my house, and we
had a hilarious and unforgettable day, working on the
game.

On the Saturday, we met for the pilot at Television
Centre. He gave such an outstanding performance himself, and got the whole team so on its toes, that the pilot
sailed through, and the show was booked.

In September, he wrote: 'I'm trying to avoid as much
travelling as possible, and therefore I didn't raise the

question of returning to "Top of the Form", especially as the same team has asked me to do "World Quiz" again, that starts on September 30th, 9.15-9.45, Radio 1/2.

'I *think* I feel better for the de-coking, but the trouble is that weight goes back on so fast! The really testing time is shortly to arrive. "World Quiz"; a weekly panel-game for S.T.V., and my own show for Thames. Everything always comes in batches!'

And, in the midst of this welter of work, he made another bid for recovery, and wrote on November 18th, 1968: 'If you'd asked me how I was on Saturday, I would have said "fine". But I've had two lousy days after a fortnight's progress. However, the "good times" seem to be getting longer, thanks (and I mean this) to a faith healer. Let's hope he can continue the cure.'

I claim no knowledge of the procedure or methods of treatment of faith healers. I have a certain respect for auto-suggestion in connection with illness, particularly where there may be a psychosomatic element. Not that there was anything psychosomatic about Kenneth, but it may explain why he was persuaded that he was feeling better. I only know of one count upon which I shall never cease to censure this particular practitioner, and that is that he induced Kenneth to stop taking his life saving anti-coagulant drugs.

The very last letter to Christine is dated December 17th, 1968: 'Health at the moment only fair, and I suppose I am working fairly hard to take my mind off it. However, I'm going to have a serious battle with it from about Jan 11th till the end of Feb. Someone ought to be able to help.

PAVANE

'In any event I do not intend to be in London during
that period, but will keep in touch.

'Hope you have a nice Christmas and a splendid
1969.'

A routine post-mortem examination was carried out
at St Georges Hospital, and a copy of the findings sent
to his general practitioner, Dr John Gordon. A day
or two later, Dr Gordon showed it to Joe Friel. The
cause of death was a massive coronary thrombosis, and
(Joe tells me) what it amounted to in layman's language was that his blood was like treacle.

John Gordon, his close friend as well as his doctor,
looked across at Joe and shook his head. 'It means, of
course, that he had stopped taking the anti-coagulants.
Poor silly fellow, if only he'd listened to me. He could
have had another ten years!'

One of the last of those gags which he had scribbled
on a bit of paper and sent to Barry Took, was a bare
two months before he died, and it said:

'It's getting on towards Christmas, and 1969 is pretty
close too. But in these days of rush and bustle one has
to plan far ahead. For instance, have you given any
thought to Thursday March 19th? I bet you haven't!
And you're quite right not to because it's a Wednesday.'

'By some quirk of fate' (to quote one of his own ex-
pressions), on Wednesday, March 19th, 1969, several
hundred people were packed into the Royal Parish
Church of St Martin-in-the-Fields, attending a Memorial Service for our dear friend.

The service was conducted by the Reverend Austen
Williams. Dickie Murdoch read the lesson, and John

PAVANE

Ellison delivered a splendid oration, an invidious task indeed, which succinctly said what all of us there knew so well about him, and concluded:

'He was a man to whom God gave the gift of laughter, and who shared it with the world to the end, exactly as he would have wished. But, of course, it isn't the end, it's only part of the whole story, and I would ask all of you who loved him not to grieve too much. He wouldn't have wanted you to. "See you around!" was a pet saying of his, and I feel sure he's around with all of us here today. This special man has left us his philosophy of life. In his own words: "Live with cheerfulness and a certain amount of politeness, and you won't go far wrong".'

Of all the many glowing tributes to this dearly loved man which appeared in the press at the time of his death, I would like to single out two. The first, from his friend Paul Jennings, which appeared in *The Sunday Times* on February 16th, 1969, and read:

'If I ever knew a gentleman, it was Kenneth Horne. He moved, after all, in a world with a plentiful supply of synthetic personalities, but you never saw that glazed showbiz look in his eye. He gave you his whole attention, his whole courtesy. And what a courtesy it was! He would go literally miles out of his way to do anyone a kindness. I knew him in the context of panel games, to which his marvellous unforced humour, spontaneous but beautifully timed, always added sparkle.'

The second, from his colleagues at *She* Magazine:

'He will be greatly missed not only by the majority of *She* readers but also by all of us on *She* staff. He

was unfailingly courteous to everyone with whom
he had dealings: not for him a casual or abrupt ter-
mination to an interview in his office or home, he
would always come to the street door to say his goodbye; not for him either a casual acceptance of something done for him, he was always profuse as well as
sincere in his thanks.... Kenneth, you were a wonderful colleague, a loyal friend, a much-loved con-
tributor, the cruel-kindest critic. Thank you for all
you did for *She.*'

Kenneth had suggested to Barry Took that Series
Five of 'Round The Horne' should be subtitled 'The
First All-Nude Radio Show' '... since the title "A Song,
a Smile and Edna Pirbright" has already been turned
down because it is too like "Panorama".'

It was scheduled to start in March 1969, and the cast
had already been engaged.

Once again I am faced with that dear old cliché 'the
show must go on', but there is no escaping the fact that
it had to. Some sort of programme had to be dreamt up
to fill the fifteen to twenty weekly half-hours allocated
to 'Round The Horne', and, sadly, it could hardly be
called that.

Con Mahoney, Head of Light Entertainment, Radio,
asked Barry Took to come and see him to discuss the
situation. What was to be done? Could Barry, perhaps,
suggest a new anchor-man? Poor Barry, to whom Kenneth's death had been a deep personal loss, shut himself
away and reviewed the whole problem. Two days later
he wrote to Con Mahoney, saying that, regretfully, he
must decline the job of writing the new show. 'Round
The Horne' had been such a very special personal in-

volvement with Kenneth, that carrying on without him would present a situation which he simply couldn't face.

Make no mistake, writers are no different from performers. They are not immensely rich. We all, always, need the money. I regard this decision of Barry's as very proper, and completely understandable. His colleagues, Webster, Mortimer and Cooke put together a show, built mainly around Kenneth Williams, which they called 'Stop Messing About!', and at least filled the dates. The cast was the same; Douglas Smith was promoted, invidiously, to the job of anchor-man.

The first recording was arranged for early March, at The Paris. As usual, Ken Williams was the first to arrive, and almost instinctively he made his way to the tea-bar. He was standing there, drinking his coffee, deep in thought, when suddenly a hand dropped on to his shoulder, and a quiet voice said: 'Hallo, chum!'

Ken jumped, spun round, and burst into tears. It was poor bewildered Douglas Smith.

I myself had a similar experience when, also in March '69, I was invited to attend a closed-circuit recording of 'Twenty Questions', for the team to meet and help to break in the new Chairman, David Franklin, whom I had never previously met. This session was arranged to take place at a small studio, which the B.B.C. then had, known as Piccadilly 1.

I too am an early arriver. I entered by the front of the house, and into the back of the auditorium which was totally dark. So, indeed, was the stage, apart from one working-light in the front batten, shining down on to a table, at which was seated an obviously tall, bald-headed man, with horn-rimmed glasses. Now David Franklin bore little resemblance to Kenneth Horne, apart from being roughly the same height, and bald-headed; but, at that moment in time, my heart too missed a beat.

I have never had the remotest belief in psychic phenomena or manifestations—and yet—I don't know, maybe the old chum was around, just making sure we were all all right.

Index

(Names of shows and characters in them are given in italics)

179

INDEX

Dalton, Hugh, 16
Dame Celia Molestrangler, 123
Daphne Whitethigh, 122
Davis, Joyce, 82, 83, 84, 95-99, 109, 111, 140, 143, 146
Delpech, Reginald, 25
Denham, Maurice, 61, 62, 125
Desmond, Jerry, 95
Dick, Major, 26

Edinburgh, HRH Prince Philip Duke of, 64, 97, 170
Elizalde, Fred, 29
Ellison, John, 125, 130, 162, 174
Elizabeth, HRH Princess (later HM The Queen), 64

Fairbairn, Dr, 2
Falkirk High School, 127, 162
Fanny Haddock, 122
Feldman, Marty, 121, 122, 129
Fenoulhet, Paul, 110
Fiona & Charles, 122
Franklin, David, 176, 177
The Frazer-Hayes Four, 110
French, Marjorie, 18
Freud, Clement, 125
Friel, Joe, 105, 106, 138, 171, 173

Gloucester, TRH The Duke & Duchess, 97
Goodale, Sir Ernest, 88, 97
Gordon, Sir Archibald, CMG, 11
Gordon, Douglas, 11
Gordon, Dr John, 105, 107, 173

Hackforth, Pamela, 144, 168
Hancock, Tony, 113
Harriman, Sir George, 92
Haynes, Kathleen, 96-100
Heavens Above, 163
Hess, Alan, 92

Hewson, Ralph, 73-77
Hill, Lord, 169
Hind-Smith, Gertrude, 15
Horne, Bridget (K.H.'s sister), 3, 11, 13
Horne, Charles, K.H.'s grandfather), 2
Horne, The Rev. Charles Silvester (K.H.'s father), 2-10, 163
Horne, The Hon. Mrs C. S. (K.H.'s mother), 2, 3, 5, 8, 10, 11, 32, 33
Horne, Dorothy (K.H.'s sister), later Lady Gordon, 3, 4, 10
Horne, Joan (K.H.'s sister), 3, 9, 12, 13
Horne, Oliver (K.H.'s brother), 3, 11, 13
Horne, Ronald Cozens-Hardy, QC (K.H.'s brother), 3, 11, 12, 13, 14
Horne, Ruth (K.H.'s sister, later Mrs Douglas Gordon), 3, 5, 6, 11, 12, 13, 14
Horne, Marjorie (K.H.'s 3rd wife), 72, 79, 80, 81, 84, 85, 86, 105, 132, 134, 135, 136, 142, 143
Horne, Kenneth (dramatist), 69
Houghton, Len, 42
Hulbert, Jack & Cicely Courtneidge, 112
Hume, Sir Nutcombe, 88

Imperial Hotel, Torquay, 72, 131
Issogonis, Sir Alec, 92

J. Peasemould Gruntfuttock, 123
Jennings, Paul, 95, 174
Jerome, Jerome K., 6

Kent, HRH The Duchess of, 97

180

INDEX

"KH.6", (K.H.'s number-plate), 108, 120
King, Edmund, 38, 39, 47, 70, 71

Lady Beatrice Counterblast, 123
Lancaster, Pat, 110
Leacock, Stephen, 16
Lewando, Sir Jan, 92
London School of Economics, 16, 128
Lyons, Sir William, 92

McClurg, Bill, 42
Magdalene College, Cambridge, 17, 19, 30, 128
Mahoney, Con, 175
Mancroft, Lord, 92, 118-119
Margaret, HRH Princess, 62, 63, 97
Marsden, Betty, 110, 122, 123
Merriman, Eric, 110, 115
Merry-go Round, 56, 61, 64
Millea, Percy, 72, 87, 108
Millest, Daniel, 147, 150
Millest, Mollie, 145-151, 163, 164
Mitchell, Warren, 126
Monday Night at Eight, 51
Montague, Andrew, 132-137
Montague, Lisa, 137
Montague, Sarah, 136
Montague, Susan, 134-137; *see also* Thomas
Moody, Ron, 110, 111
Mortimer, Johnnie, 121, 176
Moulsdale, Anne, 16
Much-Binding-in-the-Marsh, 50, 51, 56, 57, 61, 63-67, 77, 93, 94, 116, 145-147
Murdoch, Richard, 49-51, 54-58, 62-65, 72, 77, 93, 94, 116, 125, 126, 145, 146, 173

Newcastle, 8th Duke of, 30, 32, 33, 34
Newman, Pat, 153-155

The Obst Club, 20-22
The Off-the-Record Circle, 92, 93
O.R.B.S. (Overseas Recorded Broadcasting Service), 49, 57

Paddick, Hugh, 110, 122
Padell, Daphne, 95
Page, Jane, 119
The Paris (BBC Studio), 63, 109, 113, 146, 176
Pelham-Clinton-Hope, Henry (later 9th Duke of Newcastle), 30, 31, 32
Pelham-Clinton-Hope, Lady Mary (later Lady Mary Horne), 30-34, 36
Pepper, Harry S., 51
Pertwee, Bill, 111, 112, 121
Pilkington, Austin, 17, 21, 23
Pilkington, Harry (later Sir Harry Pilkington and Lord Pilkington of St Helens), 17, 83, 84, 87-90
Powell, Bill, 20

HM Queen Elizabeth II, 97
HM The Queen (later Queen Mother), 62, 63, 97
HM Queen Mary, 97

Rambling Syd Rumpo, 123
Reading, J., 89
R.A.F., No. 5 Centre, Sutton Coldfield, 40, 41, 43; 966 Squadron, Newport, Mon., 43; 32 Group HQ, Claverton Manor, Bath, 43, 46, 47, 48, 51, 70
Robertson, Max, 171

181

INDEX